WINNIPEG
WITHDRAWN
PUBLIC LIBRARY

For the People

Anelia Schutte

D1253850

ONE PLACE. MANY STORIES

HQ
An imprint of HarperCollins*Publishers* Ltd
1 London Bridge Street
London SE1 9GF

This edition 2019

1
First published in Great Britain by
Carina, an imprint of Harlequin UK Ltd 2014

Copyright © Anelia Varela 2014

Anelia Schutte asserts the moral right to be
identified as the author of this work.
A catalogue record for this book is
available from the British Library.

ISBN: 978-0-263-27746-3

MIX
Paper from
responsible sources
FSC
www.fsc.org
FSC™ C007454

This book is produced from independently certified FSC™ paper
to ensure responsible forest management.

For more information visit: www.harpercollins.co.uk/green

Printed and bound in Great Britain by CPI Group (UK) Ltd, Croydon, CR0 4YY

All rights reserved. No part of this publication may be reproduced,
stored in a retrieval system, or transmitted, in any form or by any means,
electronic, mechanical, photocopying, recording or otherwise,
without the prior permission of the publishers.

This book is sold subject to the condition that it shall not, by way of trade
or otherwise, be lent, re-sold, hired out or otherwise circulated without
the publisher's prior consent in any form of binding or cover other than
that in which it is published and without a similar condition including this
condition being imposed on the subsequent purchaser.

For my mother and father,
for everything.

Contents

Author's Note		1
Introduction		3
Prologue	1984	8
Chapter 1	Going home	12
Chapter 2	Back to my childhood	19
Chapter 3	1970	22
Chapter 4	Digging	27
Chapter 5	1970–1	33
Chapter 6	Colourful stories	40
Chapter 7	Xenophobia	49
Chapter 8	1972	56
Chapter 9	Jack and Piet	61
Chapter 10	1972	70
Chapter 11	1972–8	74
Chapter 12	Queenie	80
Chapter 13	The funeral	86
Chapter 14	1978–82	97
Chapter 15	1982	101
Chapter 16	Township tour	105
Chapter 17	1982	116
Chapter 18	Mrs Burger	121
Chapter 19	1983	125
Chapter 20	Crèche tour	130

Chapter 21 1983   137
Chapter 22 1983   147
Chapter 23 Oupad   152
Chapter 24 Tembelitsha   155
Chapter 25 1983   161
Chapter 26 Theron   165
Chapter 27 1983   170
Chapter 28 Memories of apartheid   173
Chapter 29 1983   177
Chapter 30 Johnny   181
Chapter 31 1984   188
Chapter 32 1986   193
Chapter 33 Lois Bubb   199
Chapter 34 1986   207
Chapter 35 Amy Matungana   210
Chapter 36 Trouble   218
Chapter 37 Esther Xokiso   223
Chapter 38 1986   233
Chapter 39 David Ngxale   236
Chapter 40 Lawrence Oliver   243
Chapter 41 1986   260
Chapter 42 1986   263
Chapter 43 Tapped   269
Chapter 44 1986   272
Chapter 45 Elizabeth Koti   276
Chapter 46 1987   285
Chapter 47 1987–8   289
Chapter 48 Winile Joyi   294
Chapter 49 1988   297
Chapter 50 Goodbyes   302
Epilogue   1994   305

Author's Note

Black South Africans: *descendants of the many African tribes in South Africa, each with its own culture, language and traditions going back several thousand years. The most prominent of these are the Xhosa and Zulu people.*

White South Africans: *descendants of the Europeans who settled in South Africa from the mid-seventeenth century, notably the Dutch and the British. White South Africans fall primarily into two groups based on their native language: English or Afrikaans.*

Coloured South Africans: *a term commonly used in South Africa for people of mixed race with some African ancestry, usually combined with one or more lineages including European, Indonesian, Madagascan and Malay. Mainly Afrikaans-speaking, they're also known as 'bruinmense' ('brown people').*

Introduction

I was born into apartheid. From 1978 until Nelson Mandela's release from prison in 1990, it was the only reality I knew.

My parents had grown up with it too. When the National Party came into power in 1948, both my mother and father were four years old.

The National Party government introduced a system of racial segregation that would become known as *apartheid* – 'separateness' – enforced by a series of acts and laws. Land was separated into homogenous areas for white, coloured and black. Children of different races were forced to go to different schools. It became illegal for white people to marry people of other races – or, under the 'Immorality Act', even to have sex with them.

As our country became scorned, sanctioned and boycotted by the rest of the world, it became ever more insular, our press heavily censored by the apartheid government.

I knew very little of this history before 2007, when I started working on this book.

Growing up in a small town in South Africa, I never

questioned apartheid. It was just the way it was – a refrain I've heard from many white South Africans since.

I was twelve years old when Nelson Mandela was released. Preoccupied with school and boys, I was only vaguely aware of what was going on.

Many white adults were nervous about what might happen at the time. Some of the more right-wing stockpiled food and guns in anticipation of what was surely an inevitable civil war, as apartheid laws were abolished and black people's voting rights reinstated.

At sixteen, I was too young to vote in South Africa's first democratic election, which saw the African National Congress, or ANC – for years treated as a terrorist organisation – become our new government, and Nelson Mandela our new president.

To everyone's relief, the worst fears were unfounded. Where the apartheid government enforced segregation and oppression, Mandela encouraged forgiveness and reconciliation.

The most unifying gesture of all was his appearance at the 1995 Rugby World Cup, wearing the green and gold of our national team, the Springboks.

In our living room, I cheered with my family and the rest of the country when he lifted that cup with white rugby captain Francois Pienaar.

Everything was going to be OK.

Things changed quickly. National service was abolished so soon after the election that my brother, who'd simply assumed he'd go to the army straight after school, still went despite being one of the first generation of white boys who didn't have to. He simply didn't have a plan B.

He was one of very few people in the army that year who weren't coloured or black.

When I finished high school in 1995, I applied for a scholarship to an advertising school in Cape Town, as the tuition fees were more than my parents could afford. I was told my skin was the wrong colour. I still went, after my parents remortgaged their house to pay for it.

One of the upsides of our new democracy was that the world opened up to us in a way it never had before. As a result, a new wanderlust broke out among young white South Africans. My oldest brother was the first in our family to leave, just two years after Mandela's release, to go backpacking around Europe. Having had a taste of the world, he came back to South Africa just long enough to get a qualification before returning to Europe, where he settled in the UK and eventually married a British woman.

When my family went to London for the wedding, my mother got her first ever passport at the age of fifty-three. My father and I already had passports, but only because we'd both been to Namibia – my father on a one-off fishing trip, and me for a week of canoeing the year before.

In London, I was amazed to share the Tube with well-dressed black people who spoke not in African accents but British ones.

Having had a taste of the world beyond South Africa, the travel bug bit me too and in 1999 I left, aged twenty-one and armed with a working holiday visa for the UK.

Those of us who left were criticised by the government for creating a 'brain drain' in the country at a time when it was hard at work rebuilding itself. While it's true that many people left because of the limited job prospects for white people in a country that was hastily redressing its race balance, my own motivations were more personal. I was in an enforced break in my copywriting career, after losing my job at an ad agency. And I had fallen for a man in London during the trip for my brother's wedding. The relationship didn't last, but I never went back to live in South Africa.

In London, I quickly got out of touch with what was going on back home. I went over to see my parents every eighteen months or so, but with only two weeks there at a time, I became a tourist in my own country.

It was on a writing retreat in Spain that I first started questioning the way things were back home. By then I was a British Citizen through naturalisation, having lived in England long enough to get a British passport. South Africa felt very far away.

But when I interviewed a local farmer in Aracena called Alfonso Perez, I suddenly felt myself drawn back to my homeland. Alfonso told us one story after another of the Spanish Civil War and how it had divided his country, with friends and even family finding themselves on opposite sides of a violent struggle.

I couldn't help drawing comparisons with South Africa, and faint memories started flickering in my mind. Pieced together from several phone calls to my mother in South Africa, one of those memories became a short story.

I never thought it would become the prologue to a book. My then husband, a Brit and also a writer, put the idea in my head on my return to London. 'There's a book here,' he said. 'And only you can write it.'

At first I laughed it off: I didn't have a book in me.

But then the memories started coming back: snippets of stories my parents had told me when I was growing up, of my mother's work in the townships.

I became curious, wanting to know more about those stories and the stories behind them.

At first my mother hated the idea.

'I was just doing my job,' she said.

But she was keen to encourage my writing and eventually gave in. Just three months after my time in Spain, I used a Christmas trip to South Africa to start doing some research.

It was a frustrating process. My mother's memory was sketchy in places, leaving big gaps in the story. Many of the places that might have kept official records from that time were closed for the holiday season. And without a clear contextual framework or timeline, the few interviews I did made little sense to me.

I realised if I was going to do this, I had to do it properly.

A year and a half later, I took three months off work and went back to South Africa armed with a laptop, a Dictaphone and a crash course in interviewing from my boss, an ex-investigative journalist.

This time I wanted to hear not just my mother's side of the story. I wanted to speak to the people who lived in the townships, and the authorities who'd built them. I wanted to speak to the people who'd worked for the apartheid government then, and the people who work for the ANC government now. I wanted to speak to the rioters who'd stood up for their human rights, and the policemen who'd arrested them.

This is what I found.

Prologue

1984

They call her *Nobantu*, but that wasn't always her name.

While it is true that she was given that name in a church, it was far from a traditional christening. The church in question was little more than a shack; no spire, no bell, no stained-glass windows. Just a simple room with walls of corrugated iron. On the outside, those walls were painted red, the earthy terracotta of Klein Karoo dust. And so it was known as the *Rooi Kerk* – the Red Church – in the township called *Flenterlokasie*: location in tatters.

There were twenty-two women in the church that day. Twenty-two black faces under colourful headscarves, twenty-two bosoms squeezed into their smartest dresses (mostly hand-me-downs from their white employers). Strapped onto some of their backs were babies whose innocent faces peered out from under tightly knotted shawls, unaware of the hardship they'd been born into.

There were men, too, four of them, dressed respectfully in worn but neat suits.

They were the township committees, those men and

women. Representing the townships to the west of Knysna was the Thembalethu committee, Thembalethu meaning 'our trust'. And from the other side of town came the committee called Vulindlela, meaning 'open the road'.

And that was how they arranged themselves in the Red Church that day: Thembalethu on the one side, Vulindlela on the other, twenty-two women and four men sitting on plastic chairs in their place of worship.

But they were not there to worship their God, not that day. They were there to honour a white woman.

For two years, that woman had been coming to their homes and changing their lives. She was the one who helped to start a crèche when she realised their children hadn't held a pencil by the time they went to school. She was the one who took those children to the beach for the first time in their lives. She was the one who taught the local women to sew, when their only skill until then had been cleaning white people's houses. She was the one who fought for their right to have more than one water tap serving an entire community.

For all of that they were honouring her that day, in a way reserved only for those who earned the respect and the love of the people. They were to give her a Xhosa name: a name they could use to greet her, to welcome her, and to call to her when they needed her.

The two committees had each chosen a name, which they wrote on a scrap of paper and placed on a table at the front of the church.

On the left, 'Nobantu': for the people. On the right, 'Noluthandu': the one with the love.

And then they began to sing.

They sang songs of joy and songs of hope, and as they

sang the twenty-two women and four men formed a line and danced, single file, shuffling towards the tables.

And they reached into their pockets and into their bosoms, and on the name they felt most worthy of the woman, they placed their crumpled notes and sweaty coins – one rand, two rand, five rand, even ten. However much they had to give, they gave.

And they danced and they sang until all twenty-two women and four men had voted with their hearts and their pockets.

The money was counted, counted again. A decision was reached.

The woman was to be known as Nobantu. 'For the people.'

They gave her the crumpled notes and the sweaty coins, one hundred and three rand in total – more than two months' income for most of them. And, despite her protests, they insisted that the money, like the name, was hers.

In the four years that followed, the woman continued to fight for the rights of the people through times of unrest and protest, discontent and violence. During the national state of emergency in 1986, she drove through police barricades and past armoured Casspirs, around burning tyres and past angry youths who were ready to launch bottles and stones at the first white driver they saw. But when she approached, they lowered their bottles and dropped their stones to wave her through. She was Nobantu. She was there for the people.

But it was becoming increasingly dangerous.

The youths were being influenced by their more radical peers from surrounding areas, and eventually the hands holding those bottles and stones were no longer familiar.

There were issues closer to home, too. The security police

branded the woman an instigator. Why else would she sympathise with those people? And so she was blacklisted, her family's phone tapped in an attempt by the security police to find the evidence they needed to implicate her in the growing unrest.

Fearing for the safety of her family – not her own – the woman left the people in 1988.

But the people remember.

And even today when the woman walks down the street, she still hears the cry, 'Nobantu!' from grown men and women; black men and women who were once children she'd taken to the beach when they'd never seen the sea.

They call her Nobantu.

I call her Mother.

Chapter 1

Going home

My mother is in the passenger seat in front of me, my father next to her, driving. I'm in the back of the Volkswagen Jetta with a bright-pink gift bag of treats on my lap.

'Just a little something to snack on till we get home,' says my mother.

There's dried mango and guava, and big, fat raisins still on their stems. My hands reach first for the *biltong* and *drywors*, the dried meat and sausage that I crave in London every time I feel homesick.

I'm not really hungry, just tired. It took an eleven-hour flight from London, a six-hour stopover in Johannesburg and a two-hour domestic flight to get to George, the nearest airport to Knysna. But Knysna isn't our next stop. My mother, as always, has managed to squeeze some work into the day. While she was going to be in George anyway, she thought she'd get a radio interview out of the way for Epilepsy Week, a major event on the Epilepsy South Africa calendar.

My mother has been a social worker at the Knysna branch of Epilepsy South Africa for twenty years now. When she first joined it was called the South African National Epilepsy League, or SANEL. For most people in Knysna it will always be SANEL and the people who live there, most of whom have brain damage from epilepsy, will always be 'Sanellers'. A big part of my mother's job is raising awareness of the condition, hence the stop at Eden FM.

My father and I listen to the interview in the car outside the radio station as my mother reassures Eden's audience that people with epilepsy can live normal lives. She sounds confident as she answers the questions she scripted for the presenter last night, but her answers are very much unscripted.

'People can tell when you're just reading it,' she said before she went in. 'It sounds insincere.'

My mother's smiling, alto voice works well on the radio. These days I'm more used to hearing it over faint phone lines to the UK, so it's strange to hear it resonating through the stereo speakers in the back doors of the car. She sounds younger than sixty-four.

Fifteen minutes later, my mother is back. Just one more stop, she promises. My aunt, who lives in George, recorded the interview and we need to pick up the tape.

When we get to my aunt and uncle's, I notice an electric gate where there was no gate, electric or otherwise, before. 'They were burgled,' my mother says matter-of-factly. 'While they were in the house, sleeping. And all they'd left open was a small kitchen window.'

Had my aunt and uncle still had Snorretjies, their yappy little lapdog with his titular whiskers, the burglars might have been scared off. In South Africa, dogs are man's best alarm system and as a result, most white families have at least one.

My parents' last two dogs, Lulu and Nina, were what my father calls 'township specials'. Drive through any township and you'll see Lulus and Ninas everywhere: medium-sized mongrels with short, golden hair and white chests. My father's theory is that this crossbreed of dog has developed in such dire conditions that it can withstand almost anything. 'So your vet's bills are lower,' he says. 'And your dog lives much longer than the neighbours' pedigree Alsatians and Dobermans.'

Putting his theory to the test, my father got Lulu and Nina from the local townships, where he took them off the hands of whichever family's dog had delivered a litter that week.

Lulu and Nina are long dead now, and my parents haven't bothered to get a new dog. They don't have the time or the energy to walk a dog any more, they say. I've been nagging them to at least consider getting a little dog that wouldn't need much exercise, but they won't listen.

Finally we're on the road to Knysna. I'm on the edge of the back seat, partly to hear my parents over the grumble of the car engine, partly from the usual anticipation I feel when I'm so almost home.

The sixty-kilometre drive from George to Knysna is a scenic journey through the Garden Route, as this coastal stretch of South Africa is known. Against a backdrop of mountains, forests, lakes and sea, the N2 highway winds and climbs, dips and falls.

The Jetta climbs one last hill and there it is, the momentary glimpse of water through an opening in the trees. Down the hill and . . . I'm home.

As we come round the final bend, the hillsides part to reveal the Knysna Lagoon. It's not actually a lagoon, it's an estuary, as my father told us time and time again when we were little. He was a biology teacher then, and he's always been a stickler for detail.

Situated on the south coast of South Africa, in the Western Cape, Knysna is 'the heart of the Garden Route' according to the brochures and websites, and 'South Africa's Favourite Town' three years running.

The White Bridge – named as imaginatively as the nearby Red Bridge – carries us over the lagoon. To our left, the Knysna River feeds the lagoon with fresh water from the mountains, while in the distance to our right, two sandstone cliffs known as the Heads let through the sea.

I'm arriving in the run-up to the Oyster Festival, a two-week celebration of food, drink and sport cunningly designed to draw in tourists in July, the middle of the wetter winter months. In summer, there's no need for such gimmicks. South Africans and foreigners drive here in droves to spend their rands, pounds, dollars and euros on lagoon cruises, seafood platters, quad-biking and abseiling. Or at least, they used to. My mother says they're coming less and less.

As we drive through the centre of town, she points out all the restaurants and shops that are closing down. Even Jimmy's Killer Prawns – eat as many prawns as you like – has gone under, but my mother doesn't mind that one so much. Jimmy had taken over the vet's old building and my mother always refused to go there as a result. How could she eat there, she argued, when it was where all our dogs were put down?

Thankfully, some things haven't changed. After thirty-nine years in Knysna, my parents still live on the same street in the same house where I grew up. As we turn into the driveway, I notice that my parents – unlike my aunt and uncle in George or, indeed, most of my parents' neighbours – still don't have an electric gate or even a proper fence.

I'm glad they feel safe enough not to cage themselves in like canned lions, but at the same time, it makes me uneasy. Crime has turned violent, even in Knysna. People don't just get burgled any more, they get tied up, knifed, assaulted, raped.

I ask my parents whether it's a good idea leaving the house so open.

'Oh, *Annie*,' says my mother. 'What difference does it make?'

She tells me about a friend of hers who lives not far from here who was burgled recently. The friend was assaulted at knifepoint by one burglar while another emptied out her safe. 'And she had a big gate *and* a dog,' my mother says.

They're after laptops and jewellery these days, she tells me. Gold, especially.

'That's why I don't go around wearing fancy rings and things,' she says, tugging at the ceramic beads around her neck. 'Let's face it, if they break into our house they'd be very disappointed.' She laughs. I don't. My hand tightens around the straps of my laptop bag.

My parents have never been materialistic. 'Money is nice, but it's not essential,' is my mother's motto. So although the house is big – five comfortable bedrooms over three floors and a pool in the back garden – it's well lived-in, crammed full of trinkets and pictures and mementoes that have no real value beyond the sentimental.

Even the TV would be unlikely to appeal to a would-be burglar, being so old it doesn't have a remote control. Not that it's ever stopped my father changing channels or adjusting the volume from his armchair – ever inventive, he uses a metre-long dowel and some precision aiming to adjust the manual buttons and slide controls.

When I walk into the house, I feel the warm familiarity of home.

Greeting me in the kitchen is a rusty old fridge that used to be my grandmother's. It's covered in pictures and newspaper cuttings, even more than I remember. Now, alongside a photo of my grandfather in hospital before he died, there are pictures from my and my two brothers' weddings in Knysna, London and Barcelona. Next to a faded, laminated poster of a pig ('Those who indulge, bulge') that's been there for as long as I can remember, there's a postcard of Picasso's *Weeping Woman* that I sent my mother from Paris. And next to a fridge magnet of an Irish blessing is another carrying a bible verse: 'Be strong. Be courageous.'

One new addition to the fridge gallery that catches my eye is a newspaper clipping. It's a photo of a black man in a wheelchair, his arm and leg in plaster casts. He's being pushed along by another black man on crutches, both his arms and one leg also in plaster.

Everywhere I look in the house, there are memories. In the dining room, the old upright Otto Bach piano on which I learned to play is now covered in candles, many of them gifts from family and friends around the world. My mother insists on burning those candles, all of them, when she and my father have guests over for dinner, and there are multi-coloured dribbles and drops of wax all over the piano lid.

The wall opposite is a shrine to times gone by. Antique keys, medals, fob watches and hair curlers are stuck onto the wall with putty that has hardened into a cement-like bond after thirty-odd years. An old cast-iron meat grinder is stuffed full of porcupine quills and attached to a sturdy old cashier's till. A wiry spectacle frame that has long since lost its lenses brings back memories of school plays.

But it's a simply framed cheque that takes pride of place at the top of the wall: a cheque for one hundred and three rand, made out to 'Nobantu' and dated 15 October 1984.

On a white border around the cheque are two headings, 'Vulindlela' and 'Thembalethu', in my mother's handwriting. Under each heading are the committee members' signatures.

Some of the signatures are spidery, like my grandmother's handwriting in the years before she died. Some are elegant and considered, others are childlike and laboured. One Thembalethu committee member started signing under the Vulindlela heading, realised her mistake halfway through her first name, scratched it out and started again. But they're all there. All twenty-two women. All four men.

Elsewhere on the wall, there are more recent acknowledgements of my mother's work. A Certificate of Merit from the Rotary Club of Knysna thanks her for 'outstanding and invaluable services rendered in the community'. On another certificate, the Knysna Municipality names her a 'Woman of Worth'.

But while those newer accolades are squeezed in between the bits of junk on the wall, the cheque to Nobantu from 1984 hangs above them all.

Chapter 2

Back to my childhood

My parents have given me the option of sleeping in the garden flat, which has a separate entrance from the main house. Whenever my brothers and I are here at the same time, there's a mock-debate over who'll get to stay in the flat, the most private and only en-suite room at my parents' house. All three of us know that my oldest brother and his wife will always be first in line and I, as the youngest, will always be last. This time I'm here alone, giving me first dibs on the prize room.

Despite the rare opportunity to have the flat to myself, I choose to stay in the main house. Without my husband or my brothers here, the idea of walking the short distance from the main house to the flat at night makes me nervous. Especially after hearing my parents' stories of break-ins and assaults in the neighbourhood.

I've decided to sleep in my brother's old room and work in what's still known as 'Anelia's room', figuring that writing in my childhood bedroom might help to bring back memories. As soon as I open the bright-red door, I know I've made

19

the right choice. My high-school blazer still hangs in the wardrobe, adorned with a row of scrolls sewn in gold thread that remind me of prize-giving evenings and Monday morning assemblies at Knysna High. On the wall next to a full-length mirror, there's a framed, faded newspaper ad for Barclays Offshore Services, my first work to get published as a professional copywriter. Under the ad there's a black-and-white chest of drawers and around the room a series of black floating shelves, the only remaining evidence of my black-and-white phase in my adolescent years, when most of my wardrobe was monochrome.

When I turned twelve, my birthday present from my parents was a black-and-white makeover of my bedroom, with some splashes of red ('Because you have to have *some* colour, Annie'). My father, more proficient at using a sewing machine than my mother, made me a black duvet cover with white polka dots and red curtains. He also made the black shelves and put them up in the ideal positions for my books, electronic keyboard and speakers.

But one of my biggest reasons for wanting to write in this room isn't what's inside. It's the view outside. I pull the curtains back from the ceiling-height windows and there it is, the Knysna Lagoon with the Heads in the distance.

Below me is our back garden and the swimming pool that we got when I was six. It's still surrounded by concrete patches where my dad has been intending to build decking for years. Between the garden and the Lagoon there are two more rows of houses and the N2 highway that has brought me home.

I spend my second day in Knysna turning my bedroom into an office.

When my mother worked in the squatter camps in the

1980s, she took lots of pictures to support her appeals for funding. She's managed to dig out the old slides that she used in her presentations, and I've had them printed as a visual reminder of what it was like back then.

Above my desk, I create a collage of the pictures: crèche children with dirty black hands holding plastic cups of whatever juice drink they were given that day. Squatter camp landscapes with eroded dirt tracks that link shacks made from rough wooden planks and corrugated iron. In one picture, a black woman smiles at the camera from under her head-scarf, the newly tarred township roads winding round a hill behind her.

On the wall opposite, once covered in posters of the rock band Queen, I stick the handful of newspaper clippings of Knysna in the 1980s that I managed to find on my last trip here. In one of the few articles that shows my camera-shy mother, she's behind the wheel of a minibus donated by a national newspaper.

Next to the news gallery, I stick up the beginnings of a timeline. Starting in 1937, when the 'Knysna Health, Social and Child Welfare Society' was founded, the timeline has space for any significant events in Knysna and the rest of the country on one side, and anything specific to my mother on the other.

There are far too many blanks, though, reminding me how little I know about my own town's history and indeed, my own family's.

When my parents and I sit down to dinner, I ask them to tell me their story.

Chapter 3

1970

Owéna Schutte opened the first of many suitcases and unpacked a pair of mud-caked sandals that she wouldn't be washing anytime soon.

The mud was from the plot of land that she and her husband, Theron, had recently bought. It was a decent-sized patch on the outskirts of Knysna where they were building a house an architect friend had designed for them. In the meantime, they were staying in the local boys' boarding house with some of Theron's fellow teachers from the Knysna High School.

Until their house was built, the mud on her sandals was all Owéna had to show for their purchase. Their own piece of Knysna.

Married for nine months, Owéna and Theron had moved to Knysna from Cape Town, where they'd rented a small flat in a suburb near the school where Theron got his first teaching job after university. The flat had been an improvement on the caravan they'd lived in for the first three months of their marriage, but they were thinking of starting a family and the city wasn't where they wanted to raise their children.

Looking for a quieter life, Theron applied for posts at schools in two very different parts of the country. One was in Upington, a farming community in the arid north-west of South Africa that was known for its exceptionally hot summers and frosty winters. The other was in Knysna, the pretty coastal town known mainly for its timber and furniture industry.

When both applications were successful, Theron, a keen fisherman and woodworker, chose Knysna.

Soon after Theron accepted the position, Owéna received a phone call. Unsurprisingly for a town as small as Knysna, word had got out that the new biology teacher's wife was a trained social worker. And the Knysna Child and Family Welfare Society was in desperate need of one.

Owéna was torn at first. She did need a job, but her only experience since graduating from Stellenbosch University had been working with the aged in care homes, where she organised social groups and concerts to keep their minds active. It was gentle work and although it was always sad to see one of the old dears pass away, there was the consolation of knowing they had all lived long and usually full lives.

Working with children was a very different job, and one for which Owéna felt extremely under-qualified. Would she be able to cope with seeing a child who'd been abused or neglected? Or taking a child away from his parents to put him in foster care?

Adding to her crisis of confidence was the job title: *senior* social worker. The society already had two social workers who were far more experienced than Owéna, especially when it came to dealing with children and families. Yet she was offered the senior position – with the higher salary that came with it – only because, she suspected, she was white and they were coloured, or mixed-race.

Owéna didn't know much about politics. She'd been born in 1944 to a conservative Afrikaans family who, like most Afrikaners, respected the government's authority and accepted its decisions unquestioningly – even when, from 1948, that government was the National Party with its separatist ideals.

Owéna's upbringing wasn't a particularly privileged one, not by white South African standards. Her father was a station-master for the national railways, a job that hardly paid a handsome wage, and her mother was a housewife who'd married in a simple sundress because her family couldn't afford a wedding gown.

Owéna was just four years old when the National Party, which would go on to introduce apartheid, came into power. So she didn't find it strange that there was a separate queue at the post office for black and coloured people. It was just the way it had always been. She didn't even notice the separate counters in butchers' shops, where the prime cuts were displayed behind glass at the whites-only counter, while black and coloured customers had to take whatever sinewy off-cuts they got. And when Owéna used a public toilet, she never stopped to ask why she could only go through the door euphemistically marked 'Europeans only' when she had never been to Europe.

Like most South Africans, Owéna had never travelled anywhere beyond the borders of her country. It was just too expensive, and she had no real desire to see the rest of the world.

Despite her blinkered view on the world around her, Owéna still felt uncomfortable at the idea of going into a new job above two colleagues based purely on the colour of her skin. But, needing to work, she accepted the job.

She spent her first day in Knysna in bed with a migraine.

If Owéna had worried that the coloured social workers would hold a grudge against her, she needn't have. When she turned up for her first day at the Knysna Child and Family Welfare Society – or 'Child Welfare', as the locals called it – her new colleagues couldn't have been friendlier or more welcoming.

Good humour was necessary in their line of work. Child Welfare dealt with cases ranging from child abuse and neglect to alcoholism and domestic violence. Clients came mainly from Knysna's sizeable coloured community, with the occasional case from the few black families who lived among the coloured. White families' welfare, on the other hand, was seen to by a Christian organisation in town.

While Owéna was working a six-day week at Child Welfare, Theron was teaching in the mornings and working on the house in his spare time. He had found a coloured bricklayer and two black labourers to do most of the building work, leaving him to make things like the window frames and staircases where he could put his woodworking skills to good use.

With no workshop or equipment at the building site, Theron did most of the woodwork at the boarding house where he made the window frames by hand, cutting the joints with the minute precision he'd mastered under the microscope in biology class.

The people of Knysna soon got used to the sight of the new teacher and his social worker wife driving through town with their window frames, some three metres long, tied to the roof of their Borgward station wagon.

At the building site, Owéna helped as best she could at the weekends, happily holding this here and hammering that there as instructed by Theron. The house was coming along nicely, and she allowed herself to daydream of the family they would raise there.

Little did she know that a much bigger development was under construction not far from theirs. To the east of Knysna, just on the other side of a hill, new roads were being scraped, water pipes were being laid, and one identical house after the other was being built.

Knysna's first township was underway.

Chapter 4

Digging

Knysna has been racially segregated for as long as I remember. Growing up in the 1980s, I lived in a white neighbourhood, went to a white school, ate in white restaurants and swam in a white sea. The coloured children had their own homes and schools in Hornlee, a formal township where all the coloured people lived. The black children, on the other hand, stayed in the various squatter camps on the other side of the hill where they were out of sight of most white people.

The squatter camps or shanty towns were informal settlements where people lived in self-built shacks. Townships, on the other hand, were those areas especially built for black or coloured people (never mixed) by the government. Townships, having been planned and built from scratch, had at least some services like water, electricity and sewage. Squatter camps did not.

As a child born into apartheid South Africa, I didn't find any of that strange. It was just the way it was. What I do find strange is that now, so many years after the first democratic election and the abolishment of the Group Areas Act, most of Knysna's coloured people still live in Hornlee. And most black people are still in the squatter camps.

The circumstances up there are considerably better these days, as most of the squatter camps are being upgraded to better-serviced townships, and small brick houses are replacing the shacks. But I still thought there'd be more integration now that the racial divide is no longer law. I don't know what I was expecting; maybe some black people living on my parents' street, or a friendly coloured family popping over from next door for tea. But my parents' neighbours are as white as they've always been. The only real difference is that their walls are higher and their fences spikier than before.

My mother says it is starting to happen, the integration. Apparently there are one or two black families living in a block of flats in their neighbourhood. The house prices are the problem, says my mother. Most black people can't afford to buy property in Knysna. In fact, most *white* people can't afford to buy here any more.

I don't know anything about Knysna's development, now or then, so I start asking questions. When was Hornlee built? Where did the first black people live? And why are the townships where they are? But my mother doesn't know all the answers, and nor does my father.

The obvious place to start looking for answers is the Knysna Municipality, the local authority for the Knysna area. If there are any records of how and when the coloured and black townships were developed, they'll be there.

It doesn't come as a surprise that the municipality's archive team know who my parents are. Most people in Knysna do – it's the result of my father having been a teacher at what used to be the only white school in town, and my mother's constant fundraising and campaigning efforts for Epilepsy South Africa.

It helps to open doors – in this case the heavy steel door to a walk-in safe containing years' worth of town council meeting minutes and correspondence meticulously filed, indexed and bound in thick hardback volumes. Frustratingly, they only date back to 1980 – ten years after my parents first moved to Knysna. Anything older, I'm told, has been archived in Cape Town.

Even so, the volumes from 1980 onwards make up thousands of pages.

I'm not allowed to take away any of the records, so for three days I turn up when the municipality offices open and stay there until they close, a packed lunch of breakfast bars, fruit and sandwiches from my mother keeping me going so I don't even have to break to eat.

On the first day, I'm shown to a desk just outside the safe where I pile up the relevant volumes and start trawling through almost three decades of bureaucracy and red tape.

The archives are astonishingly thorough and detailed, and I have to stop myself squealing when I realise they include several letters from my mother to the town council in the 1980s. My mother hasn't kept anything like that herself.

On my second day at the municipality, I hear a commotion outside. It's the unmistakable sound of toyi-toying, the stomping South African protest dance. A crowd is singing and chanting, their feet thudding in unison. Around me, in the safety of the municipal building, people appear from their offices to watch through the windows. I join them, peering through a gap between two vertical blinds.

The crowd outside the building is about two hundred

strong. Some people are carrying placards made from bits of corrugated cardboard torn from boxes, with messages scrawled on them in marker pen. It's not an unfamiliar sight – I remember similar protests from years ago, especially in the run-up to Nelson Mandela's release. But the messages are different now. 'We need houses' says one of the signs. 'We vote for 15 years. Now is enough.' 'The people shall govern.' One placard says 'Defy' on the back. It's not a bold protest statement. It's the name of the brand of oven that came in the original cardboard box.

A man I can't see starts shouting something over a megaphone, but from where I'm standing all I hear is a monotonous bark. Occasionally the crowd responds with whistles and cheers. Someone blows a vuvuzela.

I know from the news on TV that protests like these are going on all around the country. It seems to be an orchestrated attempt by the opposition to fire up the masses in communal criticism of the ANC government.

Although the protest is noisy, it's peaceful and the people around me soon lose interest and go back to their work. I stay for a little while longer, then I do the same.

Although the municipality's records prove invaluable for information about Knysna's squatter camps and townships after 1980, I'm still missing the information about how they came into existence some ten years before.

I decide against driving to Cape Town to search the archives. It's six hundred kilometres away and, even if I could get into the archives, I would have to request specific information from specific dates. With only a vague sense of chronology and no idea of what information the archives might hold, it seems a fruitless journey to make.

The Knysna library is a dead end for that period, too. When the library was renovated, boxes full of archive copies of the *Knysna-Plett Herald*, the local newspaper for Knysna and neighbouring Plettenberg Bay, were accidentally thrown away. A call to the newspaper's office brings the frustrating news that their copies had been destroyed in a basement flood during a particularly bad spell of rain.

Fortunately, Knysna's Director of Planning and Development, Lauren Waring, knows of one other place I can look: the Land Claims Commission in George. She worked there for years.

Never having heard of the Land Claims Commission, I look it up. Google takes me to the Commission on Restitution of Land Rights. Established in 1994, after the ANC won South Africa's first democratic election by a landslide, the Commission was part of the newly elected government's plan to right the wrongs of apartheid. Specifically, its aim was to settle disputes over land where the original owners and occupiers had been forced to leave their homes under the Group Areas Act. Tens of thousands of people came forward to stake their claims on land that had been taken from them and their families. Around five hundred of those claims came from Knysna.

According to Lauren Waring, the records of the forced removals in Knysna were particularly detailed compared with most other places. And copies of all those records, including the ones that have since been archived by the municipality, should still be available in George.

I call ahead, name-dropping Lauren, and am invited to drop by the next day.

When I get to the Commission's office, all the information I'm after is waiting for me in two lever-arch files. I spend

my morning in George reading the files, looking in particular
for any information about the forced removal of Knysna's
black people. But there's disappointingly little documentary
evidence that it ever happened. Whenever black people were
moved, it seems they were given verbal notice at best, leaving
no proof of what actually happened. For the coloured
community, on the other hand, there's a long and detailed
paper trail.

I'm soon drawn into the coloured people's story and am
amazed at how 'official' it all was. In the files, I find the
Land Claims Commission's report on the Knysna area with
all the evidence to support it. There's a memorandum from
a committee formed by the coloured community as far back
as 1959, objecting to the conditions in the proposed new
coloured group area. From 1970, there are copies of notices
given to people who were asked to leave the newly declared
white areas. And the report quotes one government proc-
lamation after another as land in Knysna was divided up
between white, coloured and black.

Then there are the letters, many of them painfully polite
pleas from respectable family men to the local authorities,
asking for more time to move to the coloured area so they
could get enough money together to build their own homes.

If my idea of forced removals was that they were met
with anger and resistance, the reality, it seems – for the
coloured people, at least – was far more compliant and
resigned.

Chapter 5

1970–1

When Hornlee was being built on the eastern outskirts of Knysna, Owéna was working on the opposite side of town in an outlying area called Rheenendal. There she looked after the welfare of a small coloured community, mainly labourers on the surrounding farms and timber plantations.

Situated outside the municipal boundaries of Knysna, Rheenendal was never declared white under the Group Areas Act – and so the coloured families in the area could stay in their homes, many of them living on their white employers' farms.

Owéna's work saw her visiting families and running activities for pre-school children and the elderly. Occasionally she had to deal with a case of alcohol or child abuse, the two often going hand in hand. But generally the people of Rheenendal were happy, and Owéna found her new job less challenging than she'd feared.

On the other side of town, however, her coloured colleagues knew there were much more challenging times ahead.

*

In 1970, many of Knysna's coloured families lived in Salt River, a quiet riverside area where over three hundred coloured families and a handful of black families hired plots of various sizes from the Anglican Church, which owned the land. The people lived in houses that in many cases had been built by their parents or their grandparents before them, and would be passed on to their children when they died.

Some of the houses were built from bricks, others from wood and iron. But all of them were big family homes with ample space for mothers to grow vegetables, fathers to keep cattle and children to play.

The families lived simple lives in Salt River, but it was home. Everything they needed was right there, including a church and a few small schools.

One of those schools was started by a man named Percy Mdala, a teacher so adamant that children should get a decent education that he went from door to door convincing parents of the fact. When it rained and the children complained they couldn't get to school across the swollen river, Mr Mdala went to the river himself, rolled up his trousers and carried the children over one by one.

Although Knysna itself was mainly white, a scattering of coloured families lived there too, mainly schoolteachers, headmasters and shopkeepers.

Wherever they lived, in August 1970 each coloured family in the Knysna area was given a notice confirming what they had known for a while was coming, but hoped never would.

Headed 'Notice to Terminate Occupation in a Group Area', it came from the Department of Community Development, the government department dealing with housing for the coloured people of South Africa.

At the top of the page was the South African crest with

its antelope and its Afrikaner ox wagon, under which it was declared in English, Afrikaans and no uncertain terms, that the area the recipient lived in had been 'declared for occupation by members of the White group'. As the coloured people were not members of the 'White group', it would become illegal for them to live on the land their home was on from a certain date.

For the people of Salt River, that date was October 1971.

In town, the coloured home-owners were also given notice to move. The government arranged for their homes to be valued and the families received whatever amount the valuators decided on, with no room for negotiation.

By the specified dates, the people had to move to the township. There they would be given new homes as part of a low-cost housing scheme, unless they could afford to buy their own land and build on it at their own expense.

Owéna's colleagues were some of the fortunate ones who could afford to build large family homes in the higher-lying parts of the township that overlooked the Knysna Lagoon.

But on the other side of the hill, rows upon rows of low-cost houses were being built in a damp basin on uneven ground.

Hornlee, or 'Bigai' as it was originally known, had first been proclaimed Knysna's official coloured area more than ten years before.

Almost immediately, the coloured people voiced their concern.

The area was far too small for the twelve thousand people who would have to move there, they said. The topography would make building extremely difficult. The damp could make the area a breeding ground for tuberculosis, already a serious problem in their community. And it was far away from town, where most of the men and women worked.

They would only accept the new township if it were spread over a wider area, they said.

The authorities took note of the request and when the township was finally built, they allocated some extra land to allow for future expansion. That included a piece of land originally belonging to a man called Thomas Horn, and Bigai became Hornlee.

When the deadline for moving came and went in 1971, several of Knysna's coloured families were still in their old homes. Most of them couldn't move even if they wanted to. The low-cost section of the township still wasn't finished, so that they had to wait for houses to become available.

Those who had been able to buy their own land in the township had other issues. Having paid for their plots, many of them now couldn't afford to build a house on it.

Families who couldn't move for the time being had to get special permits to stay in their current homes, as once the areas were officially white, the only coloured people who were legally allowed to be there were live-in housemaids. Those maids had to stay in servants' quarters, usually a small room with its own bathroom, separate from their employer's main house.

Under strict apartheid legislation, housemaids' families were not allowed to stay with them in the servants' quarters. But not everyone complied with the rules. One white man in Knysna allowed his live-in maid's husband to stay with her. A neighbour took exception and wrote to the authorities to complain, saying it was 'like a non-white township' next door. Despite the white employer's protests and appeals, his maid's husband was eventually evicted.

Like many other men in the same position, the husband would have had to put his name down for a house in Bigai. And when those men, along with the rest of the coloured community, finally started moving into their new homes, Owéna's colleagues had their hands full.

The low-cost houses were a fraction of the size of the homes the families had left behind. On the upside, there was hot running water and electricity. Even the bucket toilets were a step up from the 'long-drops' most of them were used to, as the buckets were emptied and the waste removed by the municipality each night.

But the floors of the houses were bare cement and there were no inside doors. The soil quality was poor and the ground was uneven so that water came in under the front doors when it rained. Houses were packed in alongside each other with virtually no land in between.

Next-door neighbours could hear every word of every domestic argument and every sob of every screaming child.

Whereas many families had previously managed to live off their land, eating and selling their own vegetables and keeping livestock for milk, butter and meat, they now had no space for vegetable gardens or cattle. And having to pay rent and rates for services meant people had money problems that they'd never known before.

The houses were so small that many parents had to sleep in the same room as their children. As a result, the children saw and heard things that normally would have happened behind closed doors. Marriages were put under strain, husbands started drinking, and children refused to go to school.

While Owéna's colleagues dealt with those issues, she looked after her coloured community in Rheenendal where, unaffected by the Group Areas Act, people continued to live their lives as before.

She heard stories from her colleagues about the difficulties in the township, but the reality didn't sink in. Not until a work trip with her colleagues finally opened her eyes to the other side of apartheid South Africa.

It was a national conference that took Owéna and two of her coloured colleagues to Port Elizabeth, South Africa's self-styled 'friendly city'.

As the event ran over two days, they were spending the night in a business hotel; nothing too fancy for the cash-strapped Child Welfare.

Owéna and her colleagues were given adjacent rooms on the third floor. Owéna thought nothing of it, but her colleagues knew this arrangement was the exception rather than the rule. The only reason they were even allowed to stay in the same hotel – never mind on the same floor – was because that particular hotel had a special 'international licence' that allowed it to admit people of different races.

That evening, the three social workers went out to find a place to eat. Walking along the beachfront, they spotted a cosy-looking Italian restaurant with sea views.

Owéna walked towards the open front door, but her colleagues didn't follow. They couldn't, they said. It was a white restaurant.

Owéna couldn't believe what she was hearing. With her white upbringing and her white education and her white friends, she had never realised the extent of the discrimination against coloured people. If there were never any brown faces in the restaurants she went to, she'd assumed it was because coloured people chose not to go there.

Looking through the window of that restaurant in Port Elizabeth, she realised for the first time that choice had nothing to do with it.

She carried on walking with her colleagues until eventually they found a restaurant where they could all eat together: a curry house run by Indians, far away from the beach.

Chapter 6

Colourful stories

If there's anyone who'll tell me a vivid story of life as a coloured person in South Africa, it's my mother's boss, Vivien Paremoer.

I drive to her and my mother's office at Epilepsy South Africa's 'residential care facility' in Knysna; a home where people with epilepsy and other disabilities are given care around the clock.

The home is at the top of a hill, where it's flanked by a black township on the one side and the local prison on the other. The residents, like their neighbours in the township and the prison, have a spectacular view of the Knysna Lagoon.

I've always felt slightly uncomfortable coming up here, and ashamed because of it. The residents are all adults, but many of them have the mental age of children and the emotional neediness that goes with it. I never know quite how to deal with them.

There's a big security gate that's looking worse for wear. I have to lean out of my car window to push an intercom button on a rickety post and announce my arrival to a voice so scratchy I can barely hear it.

The gate slides open.

I find Vivien in her office, where I greet her with a 'Hallo, Tannie Vivien.'

Like all Afrikaans children, I was taught to call adults *Tannie* (auntie) and *Oom* (uncle) out of respect, whether they were related to me or not. Even now that I'm in my thirties, Vivien will always be *Tannie* to me.

Vivien and my mother first worked together years ago at Child Welfare, where they were both social workers. It was my mother who talked Vivien into taking the job as branch director at Epilepsy South Africa, when what Vivien actually wanted to do was retire.

To say thank you for seeing me, I give Vivien a packet of rusks from a batch I baked yesterday. A type of South African biscuit, rusks are much like Italian biscotti: long, dry fingers designed for dunking in coffee or tea. I've packed them in neat rows in a clear plastic bag that I've tied with red wool.

'Just like your mother,' says Vivien.

Although she and my mother go back as far as I can remember, I don't actually know much about Vivien at all. It's only in the last week that I found out her family has always lived in Knysna, even before Hornlee was built. I've also found out that her family was one of those who were removed from their homes because of the Group Areas Act.

That's the story I'm here for.

I ask Vivien about growing up in Knysna and she soon puts me right. She didn't spend much of her childhood here, she says. Her parents, both teachers, sent her and her sister away to Cape Town when she was five years old.

It was the 1960s and Vivien's parents were teaching at one of Knysna's small farm schools – back then, the only places for the local coloured and black children to go if they wanted any kind of education in Knysna. The classes were big and the children in Sub A and Sub B – now grade one and grade two – were all together in one class with just one teacher.

Vivien's parents, wanting a better education for their daughters, sent the two girls to stay with their grandmother in Cape Town where they were enrolled in a 'proper' primary school. It was still a coloured school – 'I never went to a school in my life where there were white children too,' says Vivien – but it was a decent urban school, much bigger and more structured than Knysna's farm schools. The school was in a suburb of Cape Town, where Vivien's grandmother rented a big house. Eventually six of Vivien's uncles and aunts moved in too, but still there was room enough for everyone.

Until they had to move.

Not long after Vivien got there, her grandmother was told that Parow had been proclaimed a white area and she and her family had to move to a coloured township. There, they were given a small, cramped house under the government-subsidized or 'sub-economic' housing scheme.

'That was my first township experience,' says Vivien.

The next time her father visited his daughters and saw where they were living, he promptly brought them back to Knysna. Vivien was eleven years old.

By then, her parents were living in Salt River.

Vivien remembers having only the most basic facilities in Salt River. Water for washing and cooking came from springs or tanks that collected rainwater in the winter months. Toilets were 'long drops' dug in the ground. Light came from lamps and candles, and food was cooked on wood-fired ovens and paraffin stoves. But the house was big and there was ample space to play.

Not that Vivien settled there for very long. Ever concerned about their daughters' education, her parents sent her and her sister to stay with family friends in town so they could be closer to their school.

I stop her there. Until I read the Land Claims report the other day, I never knew that there were ever coloured people living in Knysna itself. Who were they? Where did they live?

Vivien starts listing the names of the families, ten surnames in total. She can still remember exactly where they lived, too, identifying the houses by the white people who live there now, or the shops they've become.

Vivien lived in one of those houses herself, but not for long. After two years her parents sent her away again, this time because there was no proper secondary school for coloured children in Knysna. So once again she found herself in Cape Town, this time living with an aunt who'd been able to afford to build her own house in a coloured township, giving her family more space than in the boxy, pre-built houses provided by the government.

At the time, Vivien's parents still lived in Salt River and she spent every school holiday there.

She was in her second year of university when Hornlee first became 'home'.

Vivien's father had died by the time her mother was told she had to move to the coloured area because her house was now on white land. Like Vivien's aunt in Cape Town, her mother was able to afford her own piece of land in the

township and have a house built on it. But it was still a
difficult transition.

'You choose who you want to associate with,' says Vivien,
speaking generally. 'So you know you get along with these
people, but you don't fancy those people for whatever reason.
They're the natural choices you make. But the thing about
living in the townships then was that you had to live next
to people who just didn't understand you, and you didn't
understand them. You didn't have the same outlook on life,
you shared nothing.'

Schools were another issue, she says. When people all
over South Africa were moved to places like Hornlee, there
often weren't schools for their children yet, or there'd be a
primary school but no secondary school. As a result, many
coloured children stopped going to school altogether.

'And so you broke down a whole lot of people, not by
making it intentionally difficult, but by not caring that it
was difficult,' says Vivien.

I ask her what the worst things were about living in the
new township.

'You were kind of . . . uprooted,' she says. 'But I don't
want to make an effort to say how bad it was. Because I
didn't really experience it as bad. Come to think of it, many
things were better. We had water in the house; we didn't
have to pray for rain any more. We had flushing toilets, we
had electricity. There were practical things that were better.'

Vivien still lives in Hornlee.

'On the whole, now that I can live elsewhere – even if
I had the money – I don't think I would,' she says. 'I don't
want to have to go and get used to new things. It's my
home.'

I want to hear more about the removal in 1970. Was she

there when her mother got the eviction notice in Salt River? Did she help her mother move? Did the local authorities help at all?

No, she wasn't there, says Vivien. All she knew was that one holiday she was going home to Salt River, and the next she was going home to Hornlee.

'If you want to know about the removals, you should speak to Ronnie,' she says. 'He's got lots of stories.'

I find Ronnie Davidson in the workshop round the back of the Epilepsy South Africa home.

An ex-principal at a local farm school, Ronnie now supervises the residents where they do woodwork, needlework and gardening. Today they're hammering together trellises and vegetable crates that they'll sell for funding for the home.

Ronnie and I go into the workshop manager's office where we're relatively undisturbed except for the occasional face peering round the door to ask for toilet paper.

Like Vivien, Ronnie is coloured – although he feels no need to make that distinction any more. His identity is no longer attached to the colour of his skin.

Whereas Vivien's family moved to Hornlee from Salt River in the west, Ronnie's moved from Concordia, a forested area high in the hills north of Knysna town.

A keen storyteller, Ronnie is happy to talk about his childhood in Concordia in the 1960s, when his family lived on a piece of land ten, twenty hectares big.

'Let's be conservative and say it was ten hectares,' he says. 'That's still twenty rugby fields.'

He tells me his family wasn't wealthy by any means, but nor were they deprived. His father had a car, and they had electric lights in the house that were powered by a stack of car batteries charged by a wind-powered generator.

'When those batteries were charged, you had light for two, three days,' he says.

Water and sanitation were less sophisticated. Like Vivien, Ronnie spent many childhood hours cleaning roofs and gutters whenever it looked like it was going to rain. Another chore that fell to the Davidson children was cleaning the bucket toilet. A common sanitation system where running water wasn't available, bucket toilets were housed in outbuildings with two doors: a front entrance and a small door at the back through which the bucket was removed to be emptied.

Ronnie laughs at the memory. To ward off the smells, they scattered ash from their wood-fired oven over the buckets. 'It didn't stink,' he says. But when it came to emptying the buckets, it still wasn't a pleasant chore.

'On the yard, away from the house, we had to dig holes to empty the contents of the bucket into,' says Ronnie. 'Often. And we were a family of eight children.'

But overall, Ronnie says, they had a good life. He and his brothers and sisters grew up playing in forests and ravines where they set traps for birds, climbed trees and ate wild berries.

As idyllic as life was for a young coloured boy in Concordia, there was another reality awaiting Ronnie whenever he went into Knysna town.

Every time he and his brothers and sisters wanted to go to the cinema, or 'bioscope' as Ronnie calls it, they had to go to a matinée as there was a nine o'clock curfew. Any black or coloured people on the streets of Knysna after nine were chased out by the police.

They ran out of town, he says, to make it home in time.

When they did go to the bioscope, they had to sit on hard benches on a gallery, while the white people sat downstairs in soft seats.

The post office was even more segregated, with a separate entrance for black and coloured people away from the whites-only door. Once inside, the whites and 'non-whites' were separated by a latticed wall that gave them just a glimpse of how the other half lived.

Things didn't get any better as Ronnie got older. If anything, they got worse. He remembers going away to college and having to change trains in George. At the station he had to change platforms, and there was a bridge over the tracks for just that purpose. 'Everyone used that bridge, white and brown,' he says. 'But in 1970, they built a second bridge next to that bridge. Then we had to walk separately. In *1970*, I tell you.'

When people started being removed to Hornlee, only some of the families in Concordia were singled out for the move. It hadn't been declared a white group area, but some of the houses were in the way of a new bypass road that was being planned.

I've heard about this controversial bypass since I was a child. It still hasn't materialised.

Ronnie remembers the day they realised their family had to move. 'They drew a cross on our gate,' he says. 'A white cross.'

His mother, for one, was relieved to move to the township.

Ronnie's mother had come to Knysna from Oudtshoorn in the Klein Karoo, a semi-desert region where she'd lived in a stone house in the middle of town long before the forced removals of later years. There she had grown up with proper electricity in the house from an early age. So living in Concordia with a wind charger and car batteries providing light, but not much more, had been a big change for her.

Having electricity in Hornlee was a big thing, says Ronnie. 'My mother could buy a food mixer.'

But there were challenges as well. For his parents, Ronnie says, the biggest adjustment was financial.

'There was suddenly a mortgage, and rates and taxes that were never there before. We used to bury our own sewage, burn our own rubbish. Now, all of a sudden, my parents had to pay to get it removed.'

Ronnie himself missed the space of Concordia. 'I felt like I was stuck in the township with nothing around me,' he says.

Many years later, when he had a son of his own, he took the boy to Concordia 'just so he could experience what I had experienced'.

There, like his father before him, the boy climbed trees, played in the forest and ate wild berries.

Even today, says Ronnie, his son still talks about that day he took him to Concordia, and showed him the life he'd left behind.

Chapter 7

Xenophobia

In my second week back in Knysna, my parents take me to lunch at Crab's Creek, a pub on the edge of the lagoon. While we wait for the pretty black waitress to bring us our drinks, my mother says hello to a coloured lady she recognises at the table behind us. I'm introduced as the daughter who's been living in London and the coloured lady says her daughter is overseas too.

At another table, three teenage boys are drinking bottles of Castle lager. Two of them are coloured, one is white.

So much has changed since I was their age.

There were only a handful of non-white children at Knysna High when I finished school in 1995. One of them was black, a girl in my class. In the year below me there was a coloured boy, a talented rugby player. The only others, if I remember correctly, were two younger Indian boys. They were some of the first Indian people I'd ever encountered, as most of South Africa's Indian population was concentrated in the Natal province on the eastern coast of South Africa, where I'd never been.

It was only the year after, when I went to study in Cape Town, that I made my first black, coloured and Indian friends in an advertising college that was still predominantly white.

Back at my parents' house, our stomachs full of pub lunch, my father and I settle down to watch TV. As my father pokes his dowel at the buttons to skip through the channels, South Africa's new racial integration flashes before me. Mixed-race pairs of South African DJs, comedians and equestrian stars do the cha–cha on *Strictly Come Dancing*. In one of the locally produced soap operas, black actors speak Afrikaans one minute and English or Zulu the next. Another soap is entirely in Zulu, with English subtitles.

When I was little, we had one channel on SABC TV that broadcast only in English and Afrikaans. American shows like *Buck Rogers* and *T. J. Hooker* were dubbed into Afrikaans, with the English soundtrack broadcast simultaneously on the radio. On two separate TV channels, there was 'black' programming in African languages.

My father finds the news he was looking for and puts down the dowel.

In stark contrast to *Strictly Come Dancing* and the soaps, I now see the other extreme of the new South Africa: a report on recent forced removals in Johannesburg. In one incident outside a church, police grab black people, including women and children, off the streets, beating them if they don't comply. I could be watching a scene twenty, thirty years ago. But unlike thirty years ago, those people aren't being removed because they're black. They're being removed because they're illegal immigrants from Zimbabwe who were sleeping on the street because the homeless shelter in the church was full. And unlike thirty years ago, the policemen who are beating them are also black.

When the news is over, my father goes back to poking at the TV. On one of the channels he flicks through, the same story from Johannesburg is repeated, this time in Xhosa.

I've been hearing and reading a lot about xenophobia in South Africa since I've been back here. In Knysna, black people complain about Zimbabweans, Somalis and Nigerians coming into the townships, bringing with them drugs and violence while taking jobs, houses and women. White people complain their taxes are being spent on giving those illegal immigrants special treatment. Coloured people complain they've been forgotten.

From what I've heard, it's the black people who are most xenophobic. And in Knysna, the tension between locals and immigrants, or 'newcomers', has led to clashes in the townships at least once in the past year.

The stories I've heard from various people in town are confirmed by reports on national newspapers' websites. During what was called South Africa's 'xenophobic unrest' in 2008, several Somali-run shops in Knysna's townships were looted and their owners driven out of the community. Over a hundred foreign nationals from Somalia and other African countries fled the townships and sought refuge at the police station. Teachers at the local schools were told not to send any foreign children back to the townships. For months, the foreigners had to stay in tents on the rugby and hockey fields at Knysna's sports park until it was safe to return to their homes.

It seems there's still tension in Knysna now.

One of the main stories in the *Knysna-Plett Herald* these

last few weeks has been about a group of African traders who've been removed from their long-established roadside market by the Knysna Municipality. The reason for it wasn't xenophobia – the municipality was planning to widen that stretch of road and the traders were in the way. But the public response to the money spent moving the traders – to a new site with pre-built market stalls, toilets and twenty-four-hour security – has had definite xenophobic overtones.

It's not that the traders are 'newcomers' – many of them came from Zimbabwe and Nigeria as far back as ten, fifteen years ago. But in many people's eyes they're still nothing more than illegal immigrants.

According to one angry letter in the *Herald*, 'These illegals are not "previously disadvantaged". They come to our country of their own free will and are now using us. They are opportunists and should be treated as such.'

This xenophobic attitude seems to be common in the new South Africa, but it's news to me. It has never made the headlines in the UK and my mother, who's always quick to phone me when a family friend has died or there's been some or other scandal in the government, has never mentioned it either.

So when my mother invites me on a diversity training course organised by her work, I go along in the hope that it will shed some light on xenophobia and how South Africans are being advised to deal with it.

The course is held at a home for the aged in Hornlee where we have a large, cold room to ourselves. There are fifteen people taking part, most of them employees at Epilepsy South Africa, plus a handful from other charitable organisations in neighbouring towns.

The course-leader, a man called Ismaiyili from somewhere

in North Africa, divides us into groups, deliberately mixing white, black, coloured, English, Afrikaans, Xhosa, young, old, male and female. I'm separated from my mother and end up in a group with a black man, two black women and two coloured women.

From the start, xenophobia features high on the agenda – as high as the first page of the handbook we're given, where it says that a recent report on migration in South Africa showed that 'the practice of xenophobia by South Africans is amongst the highest in the world'.

Ismaiyili asks us to discuss, in our groups, whether foreigners should be allowed to set up a business or get a job in South Africa.

Within our group, there's a barrier to our communication: the older of the coloured women speaks only Afrikaans. And the younger of the black men refuses to speak anything other than English. I end up translating for the coloured woman's benefit.

When I was growing up, it was mandatory for white children to study both English and Afrikaans at school.

Having established in our group that by 'foreigners' we mean Zimbabweans, Nigerians, Somalis and Mozambicans, my three black team-mates insist that those foreigners shouldn't be allowed to work in South Africa at all.

'They come here and they take our jobs,' says one.

'And they're cheap labour,' says another. 'We can't compete.'

I try to be impartial and tell them how the same could be said of me going to London and working there.

They don't seem convinced, but eventually my black team-mates concede that it's OK for foreigners to start businesses in South Africa, but only if they give South Africans jobs. The coloured people agree.

The rest of the day deals with more general diversity in the workplace. Some of the most surprising moments come when the older black and coloured delegates share their stories of apartheid and how they were treated 'back in the day'.

The most junior delegates, about ten, twelve years younger than me, are amazed and amused at the stories of a world that seems foreign to them. And yet they fail to see the parallels with their own attitudes towards their Zimbabwean, Nigerian, Somali and Mozambican neighbours.

The next day, I take my research to the library and the Internet, where I scour news reports, articles and readers' letters on the subject.

Unemployment seems to be one of the main reasons behind the xenophobia. Black South African workers are more aware of their rights than ever, and unions are quick to stage walkouts over pay. The illegal immigrants, on the other hand, work cheaply. And they work hard.

Housing is another issue. For years, the government has been building identical simple brick houses in townships across South Africa as part of its Reconstruction and Development Programme, or RDP. The houses are meant solely for South Africans, but some foreign nationals from neighbouring countries have found their way into them, usually by renting them off cash-strapped South Africans who are willing to go back to living in a shack in their own back yard if it means earning some extra money.

I've heard that some RDP homeowners have even 'sold' their houses in unofficial transactions for as little as a month's wages. I wonder whether they realise they've blown their one chance to get a house from the government.

The black families who are still waiting for their houses in Knysna's townships after fifteen years of promises from the ANC government are understandably angry when they see the Zimbabweans and Nigerians moving in.

It's hard to believe that, less than forty years ago, there were hardly any black people here.

Chapter 8

1972

Owéna hadn't come across many black people in her life. Growing up in the Western Cape, the non-white people she encountered were mostly coloured. That was because the government had declared the entire region a 'coloured labour preference area', meaning that, by law, manual and semi-skilled jobs were to go to coloured people over black.

If a black person wanted to try their luck getting a job in the Western Cape, or indeed anywhere in South Africa, they also had the pass laws to contend with.

The pass laws were part of the apartheid government's plan to restrict the influx of black people into 'white' South Africa from the African homelands. Created by the National Party government in the 1950s, the homelands were ten regions within South Africa's borders where the different black tribes were meant to live, develop and work among their own. Despite black South Africans outnumbering white by around eight to one, the ten homelands together made up just thirteen per cent of the country's land.

Encouraged by the government, several of the homelands became self-governing, quasi-independent states in 1959.

In 1970, a law was passed that made all black South Africans citizens of their homelands and no longer of South Africa, removing their right to vote and making white people the new majority.

If any black person wanted to travel outside the borders of their homeland, they had to carry a passbook at all times. And if they wanted to live and work in a South African town or city, they needed one of two things in their pass-book: either a so-called 'section 10' stamp, or a temporary work permit.

The section 10 stamp gave the bearer of the passbook permission to live somewhere permanently, usually because they were born there. To live and work anywhere else, they needed a work permit that had to be renewed every year. An employer had to apply for that permit on behalf of a worker, so that no black person could move between towns and cities without having a guaranteed job at their destina-tion. The work permit usually covered only the worker, not his wife or children, who had to stay behind. Anyone caught without the necessary paperwork was evicted and sent back to where they came from – a job that fell to the Bantu Affairs Administration Board.

Formed in 1972, Bantu Administration, as most people called it even after its name changed a number of times, was the government department responsible for the 'development and administration' of South Africa's black population. As an enforcer of apartheid, the Administration was despised by the black people and in this context, the word 'bantu' – Zulu for 'people' – became offensive by association.

★

The government's influx control meant Knysna, like the rest of the Western Cape, didn't have much of a black population in 1972.

The few black people in Knysna – those who had been born and raised in the area and so had the necessary section 10 stamp to stay there – lived among the coloured people in places like Salt River until they were evicted along with their coloured neighbours.

But the black people couldn't go to Hornlee with its schools and its churches and its community centres and sports fields. Because, under the Group Areas Act, black and coloured couldn't mix.

With no township of their own to go to, they ended up squatting in shacks in the hills around town, on land that was undeclared for any particular colour.

In a desperate attempt to give their families a better life, many black people attempted to get into Bigai by pretending to be coloured, even changing their surnames to sound less African.

The authorities had various tests and techniques to catch out those imposters. One was to check whether the person could speak Afrikaans, as most coloured people spoke it as their first language. A black man from the Transkei, the official Xhosa homeland, would never have had the opportunity to learn the language, and so would be exposed as 'acting coloured' if he failed to answer a question in Afrikaans. Alternatively, a policeman might ask that black man to say '*Ag-en-tagtig klein sakkies aartappeltjies*', an Afrikaans phrase that simply meant 'eighty-eight small bags of potatoes', but had so many guttural sounds and inflections completely alien to the African tongue that few Xhosa people could pronounce it.

Fortunately, many of the Xhosa people native to Knysna spoke fluent Afrikaans, having grown up among the coloured community. And so there were some of them who passed the language test and made it into Hornlee.

Those who didn't returned to the squatter camps.

Whereas the Western Cape had no black population to speak of, it was a very different story in the neighbouring Eastern Cape.

With no coloured labour preference and a border shared with the poverty-stricken Transkei homeland, the Eastern Cape was a popular destination for migrant Xhosa workers looking to feed their starving families. Once there, they worked in factories and on farms, in gardens and on building sites, anything they could get to be able to send some money back home.

But the black workers far outnumbered the available jobs in the Eastern Cape. Desperate for money, many of them turned their attention to the Western Cape. And when they heard rumours of job opportunities in Knysna's sawmills and furniture factories, one black man after another took his chances and moved there, work permit or not.

From towns and cities like Umtata and East London, they hitchhiked to Knysna, a long and arduous journey often undertaken on the back of a Toyota or Isuzu *bakkie*, the pick-ups popular with South Africans and especially farmers.

Those people with work permits were often put up in compounds on their employers' premises. Those without permits, however, had no choice but to join the squatters in the hills, where they lived in fear of getting caught.

The Bantu Administration van was a familiar and feared sight in the squatter camps. Raids were common, often at three, four in the morning in an effort to catch people while they were sleeping.

But word spread quickly, and the 'illegals' were good at hiding.

Chapter 9

Jack and Piet

As a white child in Knysna, I knew nothing of the Bantu Administration or its work. So it comes as news to me that one man who used to work for the Administration is someone I know.

Piet van Eeden's family went to the same church as mine, and his daughters were just a few years ahead of me at school.

My parents tell me there's another ex-employee of the Bantu Administration who's still in Knysna. His identity is even more surprising than Piet's, not because I know him – I don't – but because he's black.

Neither of them is hard to track down. Piet van Eeden now manages a supermarket near my parents' house, and his black ex-colleague Jack Matjolweni is working at the Department of Labour.

I call Jack at work, introducing myself by my married name. At first he sounds guarded, but when I explain who my parents are, he's more forthcoming.

'Aaaah, I know your mother,' he says. I can hear he's smiling now. 'And I know your father very well.'

My father often deals with Jack to sort out benefits for Johnny, our gardener.

Jack says he'll come to my parents' house after work.

I've heard of Jack. In the last week I've had a few conversations with people from the townships and Jack's name came up often – and never in a favourable light. It's not surprising. A black man who worked for the apartheid government and raided his own people's houses to catch women's husbands and boyfriends and send them away couldn't have been popular.

One woman I spoke to put it down to the attitude with which Jack did his job. He was young and full of spirit, she said. He was just too keen.

Jack is all smiles when my father opens the door. He's tall, so tall he has to bend over slightly to get through the door between the kitchen and the dining room. He looks much younger than his fifty years in a leather jacket and khaki chinos that make him resemble a black Indiana Jones.

Jack speaks Afrikaans to my father but switches to English when he speaks to me. It seems more natural that way, as we spoke English on the phone. His English is broken with a strong African accent and he throws in the odd Afrikaans word here and there.

I offer Jack a coffee, tea, maybe a beer. Just hot water, he says. With sugar. I bring him his drink with a bowl of freshly baked rusks.

Jack laughs when he remembers the past. He has a high-pitched giggle that doesn't go with his face or his size, and I find myself warming to him. It's not that he's making light of history by laughing about it, rather that he can hardly believe his own stories of how things used to be.

Jack tells me he was still at school when he started working for the Bantu Administration. He was seventeen.

He was recruited by chance in 1976 while he was waiting in line in a Bantu Administration office. Born in Humansdorp in the Eastern Cape, he needed a stamp in his passbook for permission to go to school in a nearby town. While Jack's papers were being processed, one of the white Bantu Administration officials came to him and offered him a job. 'He came to me and said "Hey, I want someone like you,"' says Jack.

By 'someone like you', the man meant a black boy who could speak Xhosa, Afrikaans and English, and was still young enough to be trained and shaped into whatever the Bantu Administration wanted him to be.

Jack says the fact that he was only seventeen and still at school didn't seem to faze his prospective employer.

'He said I could go to night school and finish my studies that way.'

Jack accepted the job. It was just too attractive an offer to refuse. Being a Bantu Administration employee meant he no longer needed permits in his passbook. It also made it relatively easy to transfer to Knysna.

As a Bantu Administration inspector, Jack had to check people's passbooks and make sure they had the necessary permits to be in Knysna. Sometimes he would go from door to door in the squatter camps looking for 'illegals', other times he would get a call or an anonymous letter from someone blowing the whistle on a rival for a job or a girl.

'What, black people would turn each other in?' I ask him.

'*Ja!*' he says. Yes.

Sometimes the letters and calls were from coloured workers who'd lost out on a job. Other times they came from white employers, maybe bitter about losing a worker to a competitor who was willing to pay more. But most often the letters and calls were from black people: jealous boyfriends in Knysna who wanted to get back at the men who took their women, or concerned wives in the Transkei who hadn't heard from their husbands for months.

Jack explains that most black workers left their wives and families behind in the homelands when they came to Knysna, promising to send money as often as they could. But a year was a long time for a man to be away from his wife, and many of the workers took girlfriends in Knysna. Jack remembers wives turning up from the Transkei and the Eastern Cape looking for their husbands. He tells me how those wives would cry when they saw their husbands with other women, often with new children.

'If somebody came to me saying the husband has left and he's got kids, then I was fighting for that,' says Jack. 'I was not worried about girlfriends and boyfriends. But I was always fighting for married people.'

Not all of the illegals in Knysna were married, however, and some of them fell in love with the local girls. Those men found themselves in a different predicament. Even if they married their Knysna girl, they wouldn't be allowed to stay without a permit. Should they try to find work without a permit, they increased their chances of getting caught. And should they get caught, they'd be sent away, back to where there was no work to support their new family.

'What about those women?' I ask.

'It made no difference,' he says. 'The men had to go back.'

And leave the wife and children behind?

'The law doesn't look on that,' says Jack. 'That time they would say the wife must go to Transkei.'

I am amazed at his apparent loyalty to his then employer, the apartheid government, and his almost blind acceptance of its laws. But he admits that it simply wasn't his place to say anything.

'I was an inspector,' he says. 'They wouldn't worry about me.'

It's an attitude I've heard from other black people and white people too, my parents included. That, back then, you didn't disagree with the government; you just accepted that things were the way they were, you did your job and you kept quiet. Those who didn't were marked out either as activists or sympathisers, both of which could land you in trouble.

Throughout our conversation, Jack insists that he was helping people – and that the people were grateful for what he was doing. The outsiders were coming and taking the locals' jobs and women, he says. The locals *wanted* them out.

I ask him how the people reacted when he caught them.

'They would fight,' he says. 'It was dangerous.'

That's why he carried a gun.

'Because it's dangerous,' he says again. 'They can kill you.'

Sometimes, Jack says, he had to run. Other times he would get the police to go back with him. But he never had to use the gun, and no one ever as much as pointed a gun at him. Knives, yes, 'to try to open the road and run,' he says. 'But if they see you've got a gun, nobody will bother you.'

He pauses for a long time. He's not laughing now.

'It was . . .' he stops again.

'*Yoh*, it was very hard. Because it's my job. If I couldn't do that, then I would be fired.'

He says people threatened to kill him sometimes, saying it wasn't right, the job he was doing.

'And I would say to them, "Give me a better job, and I will do that."'

I've heard that Jack's house was burned down twice but he insists it only happened once, much later, in 1993 when there was widespread unrest following the assassination of the ANC's Chris Hani. It was the year before South Africa's first democratic election.

At that time, he says, anyone who lived in the township and worked for the government was a target.

Jack was already working for the Department of Labour then, but admits that there might have been people who'd held a grudge about his work for the Bantu Administration in the past.

After his house was burned down, Jack moved to Hornlee, where he still lives today.

When I ask him what the most difficult part of his old job was, he says it was sending the people back to where they came from.

'Why was that difficult?' I ask.

'Because you've got a heart, don't you?' says Jack. 'You're still a human being.'

I know the shop that Piet van Eeden manages; it's where my father buys his newspaper. I offer to go and buy it for him so I have an excuse to speak to Oom Piet.

In the same way that Vivien Paremoer has always been *Tannie* to me, Piet has always been *Oom*.

I find Oom Piet at his manager's station near the tills and he recognises me right away. There's the usual chit-chat of what I'm doing now, where his daughters are in the world, how my brothers are doing and who in the family has had babies. But when I mention the book, his attitude changes. He doesn't seem happy talking about the past.

'I've talked to a lot of people for a lot of books and articles,' he says. 'The last time I did that, I said "never again."'

I ask him what kinds of books and articles those were.

'I can't talk about it now,' he says, looking pointedly at the cashiers behind the tills. They're all black.

He seems wary of talking about it at all.

'It's behind me,' he says. 'That whole system. I've left it behind.'

Just when I think he's blown me off, he carries on: 'But only because it's you, and because I know you,' he says, 'I'll talk to you a little.'

He says he'll come over to my parents' house the next day.

After his initial apprehension, Oom Piet seems relaxed and happy to talk to me in my parents' house.

Oom Piet's take on the role of the Bantu Administration is very different from Jack's. Whereas Jack focused very much on the social aspect of reuniting wives in the Transkei homeland with their straying husbands, Oom Piet saw the role as a more practical one.

'We had to make sure the economy kept going by supplying workers, and seeing that it was done on a proper, coordinated basis,' he says. 'Otherwise, if you had to just throw open the doors, you can imagine what kind of influx it would have caused.'

And, he says, you couldn't allow those people to come in without providing the necessary services for them. But, in a catch-22 situation, you couldn't budget properly for those services when the censuses weren't giving a true reflection of the size of the population. And the people who were in Knysna illegally avoided getting polled in an effort not to get caught.

'You do a census,' he says, 'and the census says there are a thousand people. But in reality there are two thousand. Now you work according to the numbers and build a school. Then they say the school is too small. It's always too small.'

He tells me it was impossible to keep everyone happy.

'Say I let people come in,' says Oom Piet. 'Then they'll probably come to me later and say we now need church premises. Then I say OK, fine, we'll make a plan. Now you give them premises for a church. And tomorrow they come and say but that's an Anglican Church. Now we need this church and another church and another church. If you make one concession, you really need to do your homework. And that's where things got messy.'

There was never enough money, he says. Funds from the provincial government were extremely limited, and because of Knysna's hilly terrain, any building work and infrastructure cost considerably more than in most other places in the region.

On the positive side, he says he feels like he meant something to the people.

'You were at once a teacher, a social worker, a magistrate. You solved problems, you served people with knowledge.'

But he realises those people might not have liked everything he did. As well as controlling the influx of black people into the area, the Bantu Administration was responsible for removing squatters from white-owned land – two jobs that couldn't have made him popular with the black community.

'It's like traffic police,' he says. 'We all agree there have to be traffic police on the roads. But they have to catch other people, not you. And that's how it is. As long as the traffic cop catches other people, it's hunky-dory. And who likes the traffic cop? We're all friendly when we see him. But when he walks away, we say, "That's the last job I'd want."'

Chapter 10

1972

Owéna and Theron saw the shacks appearing on the hills around Knysna; small structures made from corrugated iron, sheet metal and bits of timber. Doors were hardboard or rough planks. Some shacks had glass windows, found or bought. Others just had planks of plywood nailed over window frames.

The land on which those people squatted was usually unused and undeclared for any particular racial group – often because it was so uneven, remote or inaccessible that white people didn't want it.

In one case, however, twenty-two black families settled in a wooded area called Hunters Home that, unbeknownst to them, was private property belonging to white people. And suddenly Knysna took notice.

During a particularly bitter winter in 1972, those twenty-two families were told to vacate their homes. The municipality allocated an empty piece of land at Concordia for them to move to, and made trucks available to transport their furniture and building materials to the new site, some ten kilometres away. Should the families fail to move, their homes would be bulldozed – a measure entirely within the law.

When word of the situation reached Child Welfare, Owéna was appalled – even more so when she saw where the families, including several small children, would be moved to: an undeveloped area with no water, electricity or sanitation, where they would be entirely without shelter until they rebuilt their homes.

But there was nothing she or her colleagues could do to stop it. The people were squatting illegally. And the black community were outside Child Welfare's remit.

They could do little more than provide food for the families, giving them bread, peanut butter, fruit and milk powder with the help of the Red Cross and Kupugani, a not-for-profit organisation that supplied food enriched with extra vitamins and minerals. The local Rotary Club contributed too, giving firewood to help the families through the winter.

When that still wasn't enough, Child Welfare put out an appeal to the public. Help us help these people, they said. Please give what you can.

The people of Knysna didn't take much persuading. Most of them were shocked when they realised the conditions in which their black neighbours were expected to live, and more than one of them felt guilty for not having realised it before.

One by one, the boxes and bags turned up outside the Child Welfare offices. Jackets and jumpers that children had outgrown. School shoes whose feet had gone to university. Tins of meatballs, corned beef and sweetcorn, some from the back of a pantry, some bought especially. From people's own gardens came fresh carrots and potatoes. From their businesses and their backyards came planks, nails, windows and roofing. If anyone couldn't drop off a donation in person, Owéna went to their house to collect it. Back at home, she persuaded Theron to give up some of his shirts and cardigans.

The food, clothes and building materials donated by the people of Knysna found good homes in the squatter camps. But a bigger problem was the lack of running water and electricity – and there was nothing the local authorities or charities could do about it.

By law, if the Knysna Municipality wanted to deliver any services to the black community, it had to establish an official black township. But the municipality couldn't just build such a township. That was the remit of the East Cape Administration Board, the provincial government under whose jurisdiction the black community fell.

Knysna's town council had raised the need for a black township as early as the 1950s, even going so far as identifying a piece of land for the purpose. But without the necessary approval from the government, it could go no further. And with such a tiny black community compared to the Eastern Cape, Knysna wasn't very high on the government's list of priorities.

As Knysna's squatter camps grew and the living conditions deteriorated, Owéna's boss at Child Welfare, a heavy-browed spinster called Dorothy Broster – Miss Broster to everyone she worked with – desperately wanted to get involved to help the people. But, like the municipality officials, she found her hands tied with red tape.

At the time, the South African government had three different departments dealing with the welfare of the three main race groups: for whites there was the Department of

Social Welfare; for coloured people, Coloured Affairs; and for black people, the Bantu Administration.

Similarly, organisations such as Child Welfare were advised to form three separate societies – or at the very least sub-committees – to deal with white, brown and black communities.

Miss Broster had raised the need for a black sub-committee more than a year before the Hunters Home squatters made the news. But the local magistrate turned down the request, saying it was 'unnecessary' in the Knysna area.

Even if Child Welfare could work in the squatter camps, Miss Broster would have to find a black social worker for the job. And that was a challenge in a country where few black people even finished school.

Social work didn't feature high on the curriculum of the government's so-called Bantu Education system, designed to teach black people mainly the skills they'd need to farm in their own homelands or do manual labour for white employers.

Even if a black student did make it all the way through a black university with a qualification in social work, they were snapped up by the big national offices of welfare organisations that realised their value and could afford to pay them. A small, regional society like Knysna's Child Welfare, which couldn't even offer a black employee housing due to the lack of a township, simply couldn't compete.

Owéna listened to Miss Broster vent her frustrations in the office, but there was nothing she could do to help. She was white. And she wouldn't be around for much longer anyway.

In September 1972, Owéna left Child Welfare, six months pregnant.

Chapter 11

1972-8

Soon after Owéna left Child Welfare, she and Theron finally moved in to their new house. It was far from ready, just a shell with bare concrete floors and no stairs or a roof, but Owéna was adamant that she wanted to move in. Or rather, she was adamant that she wanted to move out of the boys' boarding house. A new headmaster had taken over the running of the place and every night over dinner he verbally abused the boys. Owéna couldn't bear to listen to it any more.

A month after she and Theron moved in to the unfinished house, their son was born.

When the boy got to the age when he should have been crawling, he developed a strange four-legged half-crawl, half-walk to protect his knees from the exposed concrete floors.

Owéna and Theron kept working on the house, gradually making it more liveable. In the downstairs workshop where Theron had built up a collection of heavy-duty machinery, he made wooden cupboards and stairs that replaced the ladders they'd been relying on to get from one floor to the next. Hessian sheets over the windows were replaced with curtains that Owéna sewed herself.

When they weren't building and sewing or laying tiles and carpets, Owéna and Theron explored Knysna.

They were always on the lookout for new things to show each other. A particularly pretty part of the forest, a picnic spot on the banks of the river, a hidden cave at the Heads.

One of Owéna's favourite places was a viewpoint high above the lagoon, accessible only by a steep gravel road. Theron discovered it one day when he was on his way to the sawmill to fetch wood. When he took Owéna there shortly after, it was on a cloudless night, so that it seemed the stars were reflected in the lights below.

By the time the Schuttes' second son was born in 1975, the building work on the house was finished and, even if the dining room cupboards were still missing doors and their bedroom had a curtain where the wardrobe should have been, the new baby at least had carpeted floors to crawl on.

But with a newborn as well as a two-year-old toddler, Owéna had her hands full. The older boy loved getting dirty and his favourite place to play was the sandpit Theron had built him outside the house. There he would excavate and build for hours, often joined by the family dog – a ridgeback twice the size of him – and the garden hose.

Somehow, it seemed, the muddy feet and paws would always come into the house just as Owéna had finished washing the floors. When she wasn't busy rewashing floors, Owéna was feeding or changing the baby, washing dirty nappies or making Theron's dinner.

Just as she thought she'd never be able to keep the children under control and the house clean, a friend phoned to say her maid needed more work.

That was how Owéna found Queenie, in December 1975.

While Owéna was desperate for help around the house, Queenie Mthatshana was desperate for another job. She had three children of her own at home in the squatter camp where she lived with her partner, Tiny, and money was tight.

Queenie had only recently started working again since having her children, as Tiny's labourer's income was no longer enough to support their growing family. Whereas it was difficult for a black man like Tiny to find work in Knysna, Queenie knew she'd have less trouble. Because Queenie could pass for coloured. She had done all her life.

Queenie Bambi had grown up in Knysna's Concordia settlement, where she was raised by her Xhosa father and his second wife. Despite being black, her parents decided their children should grow up speaking Afrikaans. And so they spoke no Xhosa in the house at all, determined for their children to have the best life possible for non-white people in South Africa.

As a result, Queenie could only speak Afrikaans. As an eighteen-year-old girl, she met a Xhosa labourer from the Transkei region called Tiny Mthatshana. He could only speak Xhosa. They fell in love regardless.

Tiny was twenty years older than Queenie and lived up to his Xhosa name, *Mzolisi*: 'he who is quiet'. Like all Xhosa people he also had an English name, 'Malford'. But from the start, Queenie called this quiet, older man *Tanci*, a Xhosa term of affection meaning 'small father'. He in return called Queenie *Manci*, meaning 'small woman'. To his white employers, who struggled to pronounce his Xhosa name, Tanci became 'Tiny'. The name stuck.

It was common for Xhosa people to live together for many years before marriage, and when Tiny asked Queenie to move in with him, she said yes right away. She was ready to leave her father's house.

The oldest sister to eight step-siblings, Queenie had been looking after her stepbrothers and sisters for as long as she could remember, even leaving school to care for them full time. It was time to start her own family.

When Queenie went to the non-white maternity ward of the Knysna hospital to have her first child, her stepmother was in the same ward having her ninth.

When Hornlee was completed, Queenie's father, his wife and all nine children moved to the new coloured township. They had no problem passing for mixed-race; they spoke Afrikaans fluently and a slight shift in the pronunciation of their surname from 'Bumby' to 'Bambi' made their African name perfectly acceptable as coloured.

But Queenie wouldn't follow her family to Hornlee. Although she was light-skinned and registered as coloured, with an identity card to prove it, the government classified her children as black because Tiny was. And with a surname like Mthatshana, a dark skin and no grasp of Afrikaans, Tiny could never fool the authorities.

With no black township to live in, Queenie and Tiny settled in the squatter camp that would become known as Oupad.

There they built a church next to their house and Tiny became a preacher. But the wage he drew was little more than a token gesture and his other job, laying roads and pipes in Hornlee, was only temporary.

To supplement his income, Tiny started working as a gardener, or 'garden boy', as white people called their black and coloured workers. Two days a week he walked down to town, where he tended bougainvilleas, trimmed lawns and planted roses in white families' gardens. But the gardening work paid a minimal wage and the Mthatshanas were still struggling.

Queenie decided to leave the children with a neighbour and find work. That was how she ended up working for Owéna's friend two days a week, and asking the friend if she knew anyone else who needed help on the other days.

Within a week of Owéna offering Queenie the job, Queenie was washing and rewashing muddy footprints and pawprints off the floors of the Schuttes' house.

Owéna immediately warmed to Queenie with her cheerful laugh and her uncanny ability to hush a screaming child. The boys were fond of her too, spending entire afternoons playing at her feet so she could tell them stories while she ironed.

Queenie had another friend in the Schuttes' other employee, a coloured garden boy called Johnny who, like Queenie, worked every Tuesday and Friday.

Despite having Queenie around, Owéna still did all the cooking and every Tuesday and Friday, she made sure there was extra lamb and tomato stew, spaghetti bolognaise or fish and chips for Queenie and Johnny to take home to their families. Biscuits, cakes and oranges from the fruit bowl also found their way into the plastic bags that she shoved into Johnny and Queenie's hands at the end of the working day.

Owéna also gave Queenie the clothes her sons had

outgrown when Queenie's third, fourth and fifth children were boys. Owéna had no need for those clothes any more. Her third and last child, born in 1978, was a girl.

Chapter 12

Queenie

I'm getting ready to go and visit Queenie when my husband, David, phones from London. I tell him I'm seeing Queenie in a few hours. He says to say hello.

When David met Queenie, I hadn't seen her for fifteen years. It was four years ago and we were in South Africa so I could introduce my then new boyfriend to my family. And, somehow, it felt like he wouldn't have met the whole family until he met Queenie.

My mother drove us to Queenie's house and I started crying before we even got out of the car. I didn't know why I was crying, just that I couldn't stop.

The scenes around me were familiar ones from my childhood: the rickety gate to Queenie's house, clinging to its hinges like a dirty milk tooth. The child peering through the leaning fence next door, a crusty white line of snot drying from his nose to his mouth. Scenes I'd got so used to when I was younger, I'd become desensitised to them.

Despite the fifteen years that had passed, I immediately

recognised the face that appeared in the front door. That same wide smile, the two front teeth still missing.

It was a face I'd loved as a child, from the days when I was a baby strapped to Queenie's back while she did the ironing in front of the TV, to the later years when I'd come home from school to tell her all about my day while she did the dishes.

But the face in the front door that day was so much older than I remembered.

I realised then why I was crying.

When Queenie left us, she didn't go away. I just never went to visit.

I've been back to see Queenie once since the time with David. It was eighteen months ago, the last time I was in South Africa. That time I was visiting her as a writer, to hear her story and ask the questions I'd never thought to ask before. I was armed with a tape-recorder and a notepad. My mother went along too, armed with a chocolate cake.

Cake is how my mother has always said 'thank you', 'sorry', or 'congratulations'. When our dog bit a neighbour years ago, the chocolate cake was defrosted, iced and delivered – with a replacement pair of pantyhose – before the blood had dried. Even a girl at the local printing shop got a cake the other day for doing some photocopying for me. I pointed out to my mother that the girl was only doing her job. My mother insisted there were lots of pages and she had copied them *really well*.

The cake for Queenie that day was a thank you for seeing us, but it came with another message: an unspoken 'I'm thinking of you' from my mother to Queenie. Her husband, Tiny, had died just a few months before.

Queenie's two daughters, Bongi and Bukelwa, were there with her. Bukelwa had grown into a beautiful woman since I'd last seen her maybe eighteen, twenty years before. Her older sister, Bongi, I barely remembered. She said she used to come round to our house after school, and remembered how she and my brother built forts from chairs and sofa cushions. I must have still been a baby.

My mother and I spent a good few hours talking to Queenie and her daughters, sitting on mismatched chairs around the kitchen table. I asked Queenie about her time with our family, those eighteen years when, two days a week, she cleaned our house and washed and ironed our clothes and looked after me and my brothers.

Queenie told me her story.

At one stage, she mentioned her surname: Mthatshana. I remember feeling ashamed that I'd never known it before that day.

I've been reading over the transcript of that conversation with Queenie to prepare for today's visit. What strikes me now is Queenie's positive outlook; how grateful she was for what little she had in life.

She told me how she and her family never wanted for anything, how she would go home from our house laden with food that my mother gave her at the end of the day. Bongi remembered in particular the *toutjiesvleis* – 'string meat' – as they called the venison that my mother cooked with cloves and pulled apart with a fork into soft, stringy bits.

'*Ons het nie geweet van sukkel nie,*' said Bongi. 'We did not know hardship.'

My mother and Queenie laughed at the memories of how naughty my brothers had been. 'If it weren't for Queenie,

I would have shouted those boys to death,' my mother said. 'She'd fetch them every time they started crying and put them on her back to keep them quiet.'

Queenie had a simple explanation. 'A child is a child like my own,' she said to my mother. 'So just as I carried my own children on my back, so I carried your children too.'

She's always loved children, even taking in foster sons and daughters once her own were grown.

I'm still on the phone to David when there's a knock on the kitchen door. I look out the window and see Bukelwa there with a small child.

'Hang on a second,' I say down the phone, 'Queenie's daughter is here.'

When I open the door, Bukelwa looks upset. She says my name, then doesn't say anything.

'What's wrong?' I ask her.

'It's Queenie,' she says.

'What about her?' I ask.

'She's dead,' says Bukelwa.

She starts to cry. So do I.

I go back to the phone, tell David about Queenie, say I'm sorry, I've got to go. I phone my mother at work, my throat closing around the words: 'Queenie is dead.'

My mother says she'll come right home.

Bukelwa is sitting at our kitchen table with the child. Hers, I think, though I don't know for sure. I make instant coffee for me and Bukelwa, mix some cordial for the child. I get out a big Tupperware container of rusks that I baked earlier in the week.

There's a cake defrosting in a Pick n Pay bag on top of my parents' chest freezer. It was going to be for Queenie.

It was Queenie's heart, Bukelwa says. She went to lie down and when she didn't reappear for a while, one of her foster children went to go and wake her up.

The little girl found her dead. It was two days ago.

'I knew you were coming round today,' says Bukelwa between sips of coffee. 'I wanted to come and tell you myself so you didn't get there and see all the people and find out that way.'

I knew Queenie wasn't well the last time I saw her. She didn't just look older, she looked broken. It was something in her walk, something in the way she sat down, heavily despite her small body. At the time, I wondered whether it was Tiny's death that had aged her so much.

Queenie told me how, before he died, Tiny was house-bound with rheumatoid arthritis and heart problems. She'd had to look after him and wash him, but she wasn't well either. Her arm had been acting up again.

That same arm – along with a weak heart – had been the reason Queenie stopped working for my parents many years before. Back then, the arm would get temporarily paralysed and it became impossible for her to scrub floors and hang out clothes.

It's all there in the transcript I was reading just this morning. How, in the final days before his death, Tiny noticed Queenie was in pain again. How he said to her, 'Go to Nobantu for help.'

And Queenie did. She went to my mother, who helped her with the paperwork to get a disability grant.

Once that money came through, Tiny died. As if he could finally let go once he knew that his family would be looked after.

*

When my mother comes home, she hugs Bukelwa for a long time. Then she starts loading food into bags and containers. She cries but she's calm, much calmer than me. Bukelwa should take the whole batch of rusks, she says, for the people who'll be coming to the house between now and the funeral. And fruit, for the children. She fills a bag with pears and oranges from the fruit bowl. From the freezer she gets a whole chicken and a few packets of lamb chops that my father bought in bulk and packed in neat portions.

I go upstairs to fetch some unopened boxes of tissues I've seen in the hallway cupboard. My mother recently stocked up during a sale.

When Bukelwa leaves, it's with arms full of food and tissue boxes. My mother promises to bring cake, a big tray bake for Bukelwa to have at the house for the guests.

'And I'll buy some soup from the kitchen at work, too,' says my mother. 'Two big pots.'

Not unusually for a township funeral, it's only going to be in two weeks' time, giving friends and relatives enough time to travel from far away. It's bound to be a big event, as Queenie was a pastor's wife.

During those two weeks, as is the Xhosa tradition, Queenie's sons will slaughter a sheep to be served to the guests on the day of the funeral. Until then, there will be a prayer meeting in the family home every night, another tradition. It's for those meetings that my mother wants to send the soup and cake.

I'll bake the cake, I tell my mother when Bukelwa's gone.

And for the rest of the afternoon, in the same kitchen where Queenie used to tell me jokes and riddles while she did the dishes, I bake her one last cake.

Chapter 13

The funeral

It's the day of Queenie's funeral and I'm going to the black townships without my mother for the first time in my life. It's raining.

As Knysna becomes smaller and smaller in the rear-view mirror, I realise I'm less nervous than I thought I'd be. Far more overwhelming is the sadness.

Queenie's house is opposite Knysna's only black secondary school. The house is a huge improvement on what Queenie and Tiny had before. It's made from bricks, for a start, even if the outside is a patchwork of unpainted plaster. I wonder if Tiny meant to paint it but just never got round to it. Maybe he became ill before he could. Or maybe they just never had the money.

Maybe his son Saul will paint it now that both his parents are gone. Saul, the eldest of Queenie and Tiny's five children, lives in a smaller house on the same plot and runs a busy car-wash business on the side of the street, under a canopy where I park the car.

Queenie's is the second funeral I'm going to this week.

The first was for a white friend of my mother's in the Klein Karoo town of Oudtshoorn, an hour and a half's drive inland from Knysna. The funeral in Oudtshoorn was very traditional in a white, Afrikaans way, the kind I remember from the Dutch Reformed Church when I was growing up. And so I knew exactly what to expect: a big church with an organist, hymns, a short service followed by a burial in a graveyard full of granite and marble headstones, then tea and cake back at the church. There would be be crying, too. That's why I went: to comfort my mother.

When we got to the church in Oudtshoorn I noticed that almost everyone was white, except for three coloured people: a well-dressed couple and the gardener who had worked for my mother's friend. The gardener had turned up in his overalls and a peak cap, as if he'd be going straight from the funeral to his late employer's house to water her roses.

My mother invited the gardener to sit with us so the mourning daughters didn't have to worry about him making a scene. Like the daughters, we could smell the brandy on his breath.

The gardener never did make a scene, although he did cry, quietly, throughout the service. My mother gave him a tissue from the never-ending supply in her handbag.

Today I've got four handy-packs of tissues with me. I've also got a camcorder that I bought after Bukelwa asked me to record the funeral for Queenie's family, and a message from my mother for Bukelwa to read out during the service.

My mother would have come with me if she could, but as she explained to Bukelwa the other day, the funeral clashes with one of her biggest fundraising events of the year: the Knysna Forest Marathon.

Every year for the last ten years, my mother has run a pancake stall at the finish line of the marathon. There she and several volunteers bake and sell four thousand pancakes over two days, with all the proceeds going to Epilepsy South Africa.

When I left for Khayalethu this morning she was already at the Loerie Park sports field, setting up for the day ahead.

I wish my mother were here with me. I've never been to a township funeral and I have no idea what to expect, besides what my mother told me: that it can go on for hours, that there'll be lots of singing and dancing, and that people will bang on their Bibles while they sing. I feel uncomfortable just at the thought of it.

I get to Queenie's house at 9.30 as instructed by Bukelwa, who suggested we go to the church together for the ten o'clock start. She even asked whether I could give her and a few other people a lift and I, feeling honoured at being asked to chauffeur the family, have had the Jetta washed and vacuumed especially.

When I get to the house there are people everywhere, in the road, on the path to the front door and on the grassy slope in between.

I tug at my top, self-conscious about what I'm wearing. Not having anticipated going to one funeral – never mind two – while I'm here, I packed only jeans and casual trousers for my trip. So last week I hurriedly bought a pair of smart black trousers, which I've teamed with a black and red halter-neck top and a black woolly cardigan.

The trousers are the reason I'm nervous. In Xhosa culture, married women are only allowed to wear skirts and dresses – not just to funerals, but all of the time. I knew this when

I went shopping for my outfit, but my pragmatism kicked in and I ended up buying the only thing I could see myself wearing again. I'm not Xhosa, I thought at the time. I'm sure they'll accept my Western ways.

I'm regretting that decision now. All around me, women are wearing dresses and skirt suits. I fiddle with my wedding ring, wondering whether it would help if I took it off and pretended I wasn't married. I've left my diamond engagement ring at home, but that wasn't because of the tradition. I was paranoid I'd get mugged in the township.

I hear singing that gets louder the closer I get to the front door. A priest appears in the doorway and behind him, Queenie's coffin is being carried by four men. I recognise one of them as Queenie's son, Saul.

People keep pouring out of Queenie's house, some of them choristers in matching outfits who sing as they walk, others mourners in suits or dresses. I hit the record button on the camcorder just as the coffin comes past and feel self-conscious again, this time because I'm aware that, to most of these people, I'm a white stranger who's recording this most personal of events like a tourist on some township tour.

I hope it helps that I'm crying, that it shows I belong here, that I knew the woman in the coffin, that I cared about her.

'Hey, stop it.'

It's Bukelwa and her tone is reprimanding.

Looking around me, I notice that no one else is crying. It reminds me of a story my mother once told me.

Years ago, my mother broke down in tears at a black friend's funeral. She cried and cried until a Xhosa woman came over and told her to stop. My mother's tears, she said, would form a river that the soul couldn't cross. If my mother carried on crying, the soul couldn't get to heaven.

I dry my eyes.

Bukelwa and Bongi get in the car with me, as do three children. One of them is Bukelwa's, the other two are the foster children who were in Queenie's care until she became too ill to look after them.

The church isn't far at all; we can see it on the other side of the road from the house, just past the school. But we get caught up in the traffic behind the procession of church people who are walking and singing in the road, seemingly oblivious to the rain. I take the opportunity to show Bukelwa the message from my mother. It's in Afrikaans, written in big felt-tip letters on thick sheets of paper from an old sketchbook. Bukelwa starts reading it aloud.

'*Queenie . . . my . . . my . . . eng . . . engel . . . en . . .*'

Bukelwa is struggling. I just assumed that, because she speaks fluent Afrikaans, she'd be able to read it too. But why should she? She went to a black school where she would have been taught in Xhosa, maybe with a bit of English thrown in.

Bukelwa is halfway down the first page when she looks over at me. 'Are you sure you don't want to read this?' she asks.

I can't, and I say so. I'd cry too much, I wouldn't be able to speak.

'Will you at least go up there with me?' she asks. I can't tell whether it's for her sake or mine.

I say yes.

★

At the church, I'm given a programme. There's a poem in English on the front, but the rest is in Xhosa. Except for Queenie's name, her date of birth and the date of her death, I don't understand a word.

Queenie's coffin is at the front of the church, with rows of seats in a U-shape around it. I'm shown to a seat in one of the front rows right beside the coffin, far closer than I feel comfortable being.

The coffin lid is closed; the open-coffin part of the cere- mony had been in the house before I arrived. I've never seen a dead body, and I'm relieved that's not about to change today.

On top of the coffin is a laminated picture of Queenie in traditional Xhosa dress, smiling her gap-toothed smile and looking much younger than when I last saw her. The picture rests on a wreath of chrysanthemums, fynbos, lilies and roses in pinks and yellows and purples. Happy colours.

Bukelwa sits next to me and Bongi behind us. The seat to my right is taken by a priest. It's not the priest who led the procession; he's standing next to a pulpit on a small stage at the front of the church, with yet more clergymen sitting behind him.

When the priest at the front starts speaking, I'm relieved to hear it's in both Afrikaans and Xhosa, so that I can follow at least half of the service.

He's expressive and charismatic, like those African- American preachers you see on TV, but with a heavy African accent.

He must have given some kind of cue, because the next thing, a group of women come to the front and start singing and dancing in a circle around the coffin. The rest of the congregation stand up and join in the singing. There's no music but all around me the rhythm of the hymn is beaten out in dull thuds – not on Bibles, as my mother had predicted, but on small, square cushions that look like they were made for the purpose.

In the block of seats facing us, a woman produces a white, bendy plastic pipe that looks suspiciously like it might have come from a swimming-pool cleaner like my parents' Kreepy Krauly. She blows on it and it sounds a bit like a didgeridoo. I try not to stare.

I don't know the words or the melodies to any of the hymns, and am conscious that I'm the only white person in the church. I busy myself with the camcorder while shuffling on the spot.

A dog appears out of nowhere and starts sniffing around the coffin. When it comes over to where we are, Bongi shoos it away.

In between hymns, people go up to the front to speak, some in Afrikaans, some in Xhosa, always with the charismatic priest by their side to translate. One woman tells of Queenie's final days, how her spirits were up even when she was so ill she could barely walk.

I'm thinking of my mother's message, remembering how Bukelwa struggled to read it in the car. I lean over to tell her I'll read it.

She looks relieved. 'I'll go with you,' she says, squeezing my hand.

More hymns. More dancing.

When it's our turn, Bukelwa takes my hand and leads me to the stage. From up here, the church looks even more packed. There are easily three hundred people, some of them standing at the back, all of them looking at me expectantly.

I introduce myself, using my maiden name. The priest repeats after me in Xhosa. The people just stare at me.

I carry on: 'I am the daughter of Owéna Schutte . . .'

The priest jumps in again. I wonder if he's eager to get this sniffling white girl off his stage. In front of me, the expressions remain unchanged.

'. . . But you might know her as *Nobantu*.'

The priest claps his hands together. He repeats the line in Xhosa, his voice louder now. When he gets to my mother's Xhosa name, there are gasps, smiles and murmurs around the church.

From the thick sheets torn from an old sketchbook, I read my mother's words: 'Queenie, my angel and the light of my life when I needed her so much . . .'

It's a long, slow drive to the municipal cemetery, a big patch of land bordering Knysna's industrial area on the one side and Hornlee on the other.

Bongi, Bukelwa and the three kids are back in the car with me. Somewhere ahead of us there's a sixty-seater bus that's been hired for the occasion. Several minibus taxis have been laid on too.

In the car, Bongi and Bukelwa speak Xhosa to each other and I wonder if they're doing it on purpose so I won't know what they're saying. But then, why wouldn't they speak their native language to each other? Especially at a time like this.

In London, my brother and I still speak Afrikaans to each other when his wife and my husband aren't around, switching to English when our spouses are within earshot. I imagine it's much the same for Queenie's daughters.

The municipal graveyard is large but sparse compared to the graveyard in Oudtshoorn with its polished granite headstones and its freshly laid flowers. There are some granite headstones here, but there are also rows and rows of simple crosses marking mounds of earth. On some of the crosses, names and dates are written by hand.

Queenie gets a small yellow-wood cross, sanded and varnished to a standard that even my father would approve of.

Compared with the church service, which carried on for two and a half hours, the burial is short and functional. Within twenty minutes, the priest has said his piece and the coffin is lowered into the grave.

I cry again, but not as much as the older of Queenie's two foster children, who sobs hysterically until she faints.

In the confused commotion that follows, a woman rushes up to me with outstretched arms. For a moment I think she's going to hug me, but instead she grabs the lapels of my cardigan and pulls them towards each other, almost violently.

I look down and realise my cardigan had fallen open to reveal my shoulders on either side of my halter-neck top. I'm vaguely aware that the Catholic Church frowns on naked shoulders. But this isn't a Catholic funeral. Confused and embarrassed, I button up my cardigan.

After the burial we go back to Queenie's house. At the gate, there's a plastic tub of water with a towel draped over it.

'You have to wash your hands,' says Bukelwa.

'Why do you do this?' I ask her as I dip my hands in the tub. 'Is it symbolic?'

'Well, you touched that sand, didn't you?' says Bukelwa. 'At the grave.' I wonder whether that means it's superstition or just hygiene, but I don't ask.

On the other side of the gate there's a large bowl of cooked sweetcorn kernels. Most of the adults take a handful of the kernels and a glass of what looks like cordial, and the children get biscuits from a tray. My stomach is groaning and I desperately want a biscuit but take just a glass of cordial.

At the bottom of the pathway, two women are handing out polystyrene takeaway containers. There must be about two hundred people around me all tucking in to whatever the contents are. I'm about to take one when Bukelwa finds me and leads me into the house where she sits me down at a long table.

Most of the other seats are taken, mainly by the various priests from the funeral service, the ones who sat on stage. Bukelwa leaves me there and reappears with one of the polystyrene containers. Inside it there's a strip of meat that I assume came from the sheep Queenie's sons had slaughtered, with some rice and salads. It smells delicious.

No one else at the table gets a container and I poke at the food awkwardly, not wanting to offend anyone by starting to eat but not wanting the sounds from my stomach to draw any more attention to me either.

When the priests finally get their food, it's a whole tray of fried chicken. They pass it around the table, along with big bowls of rice and salads. I'm even more self-conscious of my polystyrene container now.

I wish my mother were here to make conversation.

I finish my mutton and make my excuses.

In the kitchen, a few women are standing around talking. I join them, smiling awkwardly until finally a smartly dressed woman comes over to introduce herself as Queenie's sister's daughter. Her name is Linda and she tells me she sometimes came to our house after school when Queenie was working.

But beyond that we have nothing in common and the conversation soon trickles and runs out.

Outside, the crowd is thinning out and I decide it's time to leave.

On my way out, an elderly priest stops me. He takes my hand and thanks me for coming. I smile back at him but am glad when he lets me go.

At the top of the path, I look back at the remaining huddles of people on the grass. The dog from the church is running between them, licking at the polystyrene containers that litter the ground.

When I turn around and walk away, I feel sad and self-conscious and embarrassed, all at once.

It's not that I wasn't made to feel welcome.

I just don't belong here.

Chapter 14

1978–82

With Queenie to help around the house, Owéna could think about earning her own income again.

Theron's salary only went so far and their eldest was in his first year of school, bringing all new expenses like school fees and uniforms.

A friend suggested selling a popular brand of cookware. All Owéna had to do was go to people's houses for ladies' get-togethers, much like Tupperware parties, where she would cook a meal to demonstrate the efficiency of the heavy-bottomed pots and pans. On every sale, she would get a commission. Owéna was sold.

The cooking parties took her to homes across town. The cookware didn't come cheap, and having a full set had become a status symbol of sorts for ladies who entertained. And so she found herself mainly in the more upmarket neighbourhoods with names like Leisure Island and Paradise, where she cooked steaks, meatballs and vegetables for well-heeled ladies.

But her customers weren't exclusively white. She also got

invitations from Hornlee and New Horizons, the coloured township near Plettenberg Bay, the next seaside town along from Knysna.

Owéna thought nothing of going to the coloured townships to demonstrate her products. Her customers in those areas, usually teachers or teachers' wives, lived in homes as large and neat as those on Owéna's own street, and as far as she was concerned, a coloured woman's money was just as good as any white woman's.

Theron didn't mind her doing those parties either, but he didn't like her driving around those areas by herself at night. So he insisted on dropping her off and collecting her again, waiting for the phone call from New Horizons or Hornlee to let him know she was all packed up and ready to come home.

Owéna did her cookware demonstrations once or twice a week and made a steady income. But much as she enjoyed it, after three years of cooking the same meals and making the same small talk she was getting bored.

So when Miss Broster phoned in 1981 to talk about a community project for Child Welfare, Owéna was both relieved and excited.

The project would be based in The Crags, a remote area with a small coloured community, not too dissimilar to Rheenendal where Owéna had worked before. A local brick factory provided work for the people but, being so isolated, they didn't have any recreational facilities or opportunities for mental stimulation. Owéna's job would be to start some activities, like a women's crafts group and a crèche.

Owéna said she'd think about it, but she'd already made up her mind. All she needed to do was convince Theron that it was a good idea.

Theron was sceptical about the job offer at first. The project would take Owéna away from home for long days at a time, and their daughter was barely three.

But he could see how much Owéna wanted it, and she made a convincing argument. It was only for a month. Their boys were both at school. Their daughter could go to playschool. If Theron could collect the children after school and take the boys to their rugby and tennis practice, it wouldn't be a problem. And Queenie could help to mind them on Tuesdays and Fridays.

Theron gave in and Owéna took the job.

But she soon regretted her decision.

The Crags was sixty kilometres from Knysna, which meant she had to leave home early in the morning and often only got back late at night. She was exhausted and her daughter didn't take the separation well, spending most of her mornings at playschool in tears.

Owéna was glad when the month was over. Never again, she said and went back to selling cookware.

Owéna still missed Child Welfare sometimes, especially in the slow months. While a successful cooking party could earn her a decent commission, she was still only doing two or three of them a week. The money she got was already barely enough to supplement Theron's teacher's income, and she knew she'd eventually run out of new customers in her small market, not helped by the cookware's lifetime guarantee.

Theron made some extra money from making wooden serving plates that he sometimes sold at a local craft shop, but more often than not Owéna kept them or commissioned them as birthday gifts for family and friends.

Like Theron, Owéna had a hobby that she could turn

into some extra cash. Using the same salt playdough that she made for her daughter to keep her entertained on rainy days, she started making ornaments of stubby little men with wire glasses and women with cherubic curls. Come Christmas, she added painted stars and hearts to her collection, which she sold at the same craft shop that stocked Theron's plates.

All of those things helped the Schuttes get by, but Owéna's unpredictable income meant some months were tougher than others.

Then, one day in 1982, Miss Broster phoned again.

Chapter 15

1982

Owéna listened to Miss Broster's proposition.

A young woman called Paula Witney who was new to Knysna wanted to start a crèche in the Flenterlokasie squatter camp. The idea had come about when Paula realised her maid's children had no one to look after them while their mother was at work. But Paula's background was in computers and, although she had a small child of her own, she had never run anything like a playgroup or a crèche before. That was where Miss Broster thought Owéna could help.

Owéna wasn't so sure. Her daughter was barely four, and after what had happened with the project in The Crags, she didn't want to leave her at playschool again.

That night, she brought it up with Theron.

It was only three mornings a week and nowhere near as far away as The Crags. Flenterlokasie was just on the other side of the hill. She could take their daughter along. It was voluntary work, but it could lead to something more stable, maybe even a part-time job back at Child Welfare. Until then, she could carry on selling cookware to bring in extra money.

Theron was quietly supportive, knowing if Owéna wanted to do something, nothing he could say would change her mind.

The following week Owéna went to Flenterlokasie in her rusty Peugeot station wagon, her four-year-old daughter buckled in next to her.

Owéna wasn't entirely unfamiliar with the squatter camps. At the end of every Tuesday and Friday she or Theron dropped Queenie off in Nekkies to the east of Knysna and Johnny in Dam-se-Bos just further on.

Flenterlokasie was in a different cluster of squatter camps further to the west.

Owéna had no trouble finding the Red Church, its terracotta-coloured walls setting it apart from the metal and wood shacks around it. She and her daughter were greeted at their car by a little black girl with tight black plaits and a big white smile. As if it were the most natural thing in the world, the black girl took Owéna's daughter by the hand and led her to a patch of dirt where a game of ring a ring o' roses was underway.

Inside the church, Owéna found Paula Witney.

Paula elaborated on the story Miss Broster had told Owéna on the phone. Like most white people, Paula employed a maid a few days a week. But whereas other white people didn't question their workers' circumstances, Paula was shocked to find out that on the days her maid was working for her, she was leaving her three small children at home with only their eight-year-old brother to look after them.

Paula couldn't bear the thought of those babies being in the care of a child who wouldn't know to dress them warmly when it got cold, or to keep an eye on them around the wood-burning stove. And with no phones in the squatter camps, their mother had no way of contacting them to make sure they were OK. If something happened to them, she wouldn't know about it until she got home. That was why Paula had brought up the idea of a crèche with Miss Broster, although she never thought she would be the one running it. With Owéna and her experience of welfare issues to help, however, it became a less daunting task.

The Flenterlokasie crèche was basic, with only the most rudimentary toys and equipment compared to Stepping Stones, the kitted-out play school for white children where Owéna's daughter would be going soon. In contrast to Stepping Stones with its jungle gyms, swings and climbing frames, the black crèche had only a hard dirt clearing for a playground. And where Stepping Stones had qualified nursery teachers, Paula and Owéna had no experience except for raising their own children. At the very least, the black children would be looked after and fed at the crèche, and their mothers were grateful for the service.

Owéna went home on that first day with a head full of ideas and a very tired daughter.

Word of the new crèche spread and it wasn't long before more than sixty children were packed into the Red Church three mornings a week. Children came not only from Flenterlokasie but also from neighbouring squatter camps, some of them as far as ten kilometres away. Few black parents owned cars, and so every morning before the crèche started, Paula and Owéna drove around the squatter camps collecting the children from further away.

With donated toys and materials, Owéna and Paula showed the children how to draw, count and tell colours apart. Paula always had a box of tissues handy and as the children finger-painted and played, she walked around wiping their snotty noses.

Owéna and Paula made sure the children were fed too, taking along bags of fortified biscuits and buckets of vitamin-enriched juice drink. Eventually black mothers and grandmothers volunteered to help, and in the colder months they made soya and vegetable soups from ingredients bought by Child Welfare.

Owéna continued to take her daughter with her and they soon became a familiar sight in the squatter camps, the social worker with her little girl. As they drove to the crèche, women carrying containers of water on their heads waved at them with their free hands. Children ran after the car shouting and shoving each other in the hope of getting a spare biscuit. Pigs and goats shuffled out of the way.

At the Red Church, Owéna's daughter joined in the songs and games, always hand in hand with Paulina, the girl she'd met on the first day. It didn't matter that they didn't speak the same language. They were just two friends, playing together. Although the colour of Owéna's daughter's skin wasn't an issue, her blond bob fascinated the black children, especially the way it bounced when she jumped. They came up to her three, four at a time, touching her hair and giggling.

At the end of each morning, Owéna and her daughter said goodbye to the crèche children and went back home to the other side of the hill.

Chapter 16

Township tour

Going to the crèche with my mother is one of my earliest memories. As far as I was concerned, back then, it was just a fun day out.

The memories are snippets, like a trailer for a film. In one scene I'm sitting next to my mother in the bakkie, waving like Queen Elizabeth to the black kids running alongside us in the road. In another I'm at the centre of a small black crowd, the children scrambling over each other to touch my hair.

I remember the snacks especially. Whenever my mother took me to the crèche I would get Kupugani biscuits: basic digestives that I now know were enriched with all kinds of vitamins and minerals, but back then just saw as a sweet treat. Then there were the airy, luminous orange puffs that were the consistency of polystyrene packing beans and, in retrospect, not much tastier. But like the black children who were given the treats on special outings, I wasn't the most discerning four year old.

Sadly, I don't have any photos from my days at the crèche.

As far as I know there was only ever one picture taken of me with the black children, on a ferry trip on the Knysna Lagoon. But when I was older, I went through all my old photos and cut them up to make collages in my album. When I got to the ferry photo I cut out all of the black children around me, except for one boy whose head can just about be made out in the background.

When my mother suggests an impromptu tour of the townships and squatter camps, I jump at the chance to relive those days. My father isn't particularly happy that we're going, two women alone, to the township on a Saturday afternoon. But he isn't unhappy enough to go with us, either. 'Just be careful,' he mumbles before we leave.

On the way to the black residential areas we pass Hornlee, the original coloured township.

'There are some white people living there now,' my mother says.

I'm surprised. Somehow I always thought that, in post-apartheid South Africa, the coloured people would move to the white areas, not the other way round.

'Knysna's become too expensive,' my mother says. 'Lots of white people can't afford to buy houses in town any more.'

'Are there many coloured people living in town?' I ask.

'Some,' she says. 'Some black people too, those who have the money. But Hornlee is still more affordable, so lots of people have chosen to stay put. Some black people have moved to Hornlee too, from the townships.'

She points at the rear-view mirror. 'Just look at the amazing view they've got.'

I look back and it's true, a house on the right side of Hornlee has the kind of view you usually only see in water-colours in Knysna's many galleries. And the people of

Hornlee have made the most of it. Facing Knysna and its lagoon in the distance there are big houses, some two storeys, some three, with balconies and barbecue areas. Many of those houses have been there since the earliest days of the township, many more have been added since. It's where Vivien lives, and Ronnie too.

Behind them in the Bigai basin, I know there are still some of the original, low-cost houses. But a long wall covered in murals and graffiti obscures the view.

'There's netball in Hornlee,' my mother says. 'Why don't you see if you can play there?'

Before I came over, I told my mother I'd like to join a netball team while I was here. I'd been playing in London and wanted to keep it up to stay fit.

I'd assumed there'd be an official Knysna women's netball team practising down at Loerie Park. The idea of playing in Hornlee, however, never crossed my mind. So why does it make me so uncomfortable?

I mumble an excuse: let's wait and see.

The shacks start just after the turn-off to Hornlee, bordering the N2 highway on both sides. Two black men dart across the road, dodging cars and trucks on the dual carriageway. There's a particularly gruesome bit of road kill on the double lines: a dog, or what's left of it.

The squatter camp on the right is Oupad ('old road'), where Queenie lived many years ago. It's named after a narrow stretch of road that runs through it, now just a potholed bit of Tarmac that used to be the old N2 before the new highway was built.

Further on, there's a noisy crowd in the road. Police have cordoned off a section of one of the highway lanes, caging in a group of toyi-toying protestors to limit the disruption to the traffic. I can just make out one of the hand-written placards as we drive past: 'We want electricity.' I'm guessing they're from Oupad, as it's still a squatter camp rather than a township.

When we turn off the motorway towards the townships, my mother tells me to lock my door, 'just to be on the safe side'. We're highly unlikely to be carjacked in Knysna, as so many people are in bigger cities like Johannesburg, but an unlocked car door or an open window is still an invitation to reach in and grab a handbag or a mobile phone.

I'm surprised to find I haven't locked my door already. It used to be second nature when I lived in Cape Town and Durban: open the door, get in, and lock the door while closing it in one, smooth movement. Then, when driving, always put handbags and shopping on the floor, never on the passenger seat.

In Johannesburg, you're advised not to stop at red traffic lights at night, especially not if you're a lone female driver. I've only driven in Jo'burg at night once in my life, about ten years ago. I did end up driving through a red light when I was absolutely certain there were no other cars coming. I was terrified.

My mother has one quick stop to make, at the Sanlam Mall, named after the insurer that sponsors it.

The 'mall' is a dirt clearing with a few small, randomly arranged buildings. 'Nekkies Sports Bar' it says on one of the buildings, twice. The one sign is sponsored by Coca-Cola, the other by Carling Black Label beer. The mall is bustling. Somewhere someone is playing African drums while someone else blows a vuvuzela. Red-eyed men stumble out of the sports bar. Children run around in the dirt.

It reminds me of Marrakech, where I spent my honeymoon.

The sounds, the smells, the disconcerting commotion. But while I was happy to walk around Marrakech, here I'm too nervous to get out of the car. Maybe it's because the people in Marrakech, being a Muslim nation, weren't drunk. It felt safer.

My mother is here to collect money from a woman who has spent the day selling helium balloons to raise funds for Epilepsy South Africa. The woman is impossible to miss. Smartly dressed in ethnic prints, she's sitting on a plastic chair in the middle of the clearing with a huge bunch of yellow, red, green and purple balloons bobbing above her head. Cola- and grape-flavoured lollipops are tied to the ends of the strings in her hand, cleverly providing both the weight necessary to hold the balloons down and some added appeal for the children eyeing the balloons from afar.

My mother gets out of the car but I stay put, double-checking that my door is locked and kicking my handbag further under my seat. From the safety of the car, I take in the surroundings and realise that some of the 'buildings' are actually shipping containers. Each long, metal container is open at one end, revealing a neat little room from which young entrepreneurs trade their wares.

From one of the containers, a man is selling tyres of varying roadworthiness. It reminds me of an old infomercial on TV that demonstrated how you should be able to fit a matchstick in the tread of a tyre if it has enough grip. I can't imagine many of the tyres in that container passing the matchstick-test.

The container next to the tyre-seller is a makeshift barbershop, complete with chairs and mirrors. Faded magazine clippings on the walls show close-ups of black men in puffer jackets and dark glasses showing off their new hairstyles. One has a lightning bolt shaved into the short-cropped hair on his temple.

Near the containers is an even smaller metal structure covered in branding for one of the big mobile phone networks. 'Community Service Phone Shop', it says on the front. Through the open door I can see a display of mobile phones, as neatly arranged as in any 'proper' shop.

My mother comes back to the car, indicating with a circular motion of her hand that I should wind down the window, even though all it takes is the push of a button.

'Have you got any scissors?' she asks. 'Maybe some nail clippers? There's a child who wants to buy a balloon and the strings are all tangled together.'

I don't have anything, but there's no need after all. The balloon woman has picked a shard of broken beer bottle off the ground and is using it to saw through the string. Once free, the balloon gets its lollipop tied back onto it. The child doesn't seem to mind the frayed string and hands over his money.

By the time my mother gets back in the car, I've wound my window up again. She stuffs a plastic bag of notes and coins in the glovebox.

'She had to drop the price,' my mother says. 'The township children can't afford five rand.'

We resume our tour.

The main road towards the townships is tarred and smooth, nothing like the eroded dirt track that I remember from my childhood. But when we turn in to Dam-se-Bos, the next squatter camp on the way, we're right back onto the dirt roads of old.

My mother expertly manoeuvres the car around potholes

and ditches. On the side of the road, deep arteries have been eaten into the ground by years of rain and water from left-open taps.

Every so often we have to stop to let a pig cross the road, sometimes it's a cow. There are dogs everywhere and I see at least four Lulus and Ninas.

I watch the men stumbling down the road and to me they look like drunks and criminals, people capable of robbery and assault, maybe even rape.

'Shame, that poor guy's crippled,' says my mother, pointing at a man on crutches. I feel ashamed of my prejudice.

Judging by the state of the roads and most of the houses in Dam-se-Bos, you could almost believe it's thirty years ago. There are a few significant signs, however, that things have moved on. Like the big, mostly green sports field that Dam-se-Bos now overlooks.

My mother reminds me that the sports field used to be Knysna's rubbish dump in the 1980s, when it was right in the middle of the growing squatter community. She remembers it in all its stinking detail.

The huge tip was regularly topped up with rubbish that got dumped on the decaying waste below. The municipality's plan had been to cover the tip with soil every day, but there was never enough available. With nothing to mask it, the stench from the tip was unbearable – as were the flies it attracted. On hot days the people of Dam-se-Bos had to stay indoors, unless they could stand the flies buzzing around their faces. Wet days were no better, as the waste washed down the dirt roads in stinking rivulets and ended up on the doorsteps of the shacks in the lower-lying areas.

Back then, new people still moved to the area despite the tip; some of them even moved because of it. Every day there were men, women and children scouring the mounds of waste for anything useful, while their pigs snorted through the rubbish rooting out whatever was edible.

After three years of fighting to have the dump moved, my mother finally convinced the municipality to act. In the short term, they made the dump more hygienic until it was eventually turned into the sports field in front of us now.

Next to the sports field, there's a new community centre with Romanesque pillars that looks strangely out of place next to the neighbouring shacks. There's even a small branch of a national bank on the side of the road, next to another tyre-seller in a shipping container.

'Aren't they clever?' says my mother, pointing at a shipping container and beaming as if the entrepreneur inside were her own child.

If Dam-se-Bos still has a long way to go, the other side of the main road is a very different story. Khayalethu was Knysna's first black township, built by the government in the late 1980s. It had tarred roads from the start, before any houses were built, and those same roads are still in pretty good condition.

Some of the original Khayalethu houses are still standing, wooden houses on stilts that are small and basic but neat compared with the DIY shacks of Dam-se-Bos. Dotted among them are boxy brick houses, some finished, others waiting for windows, plaster and paint, but all of them identical in shape and size.

'Those are the RDP houses,' my mother says. 'They're the ones the ANC government are building.'

My mother says the original RDP houses were just two rooms and a bathroom. But some people have already started building on extensions to create more space and make the homes their own. The basic house is made of brick, so at least it won't burn to the ground at the drop of a candle, like the wooden shacks do.

I've heard from a surveyor friend that the newer RDP houses have two bedrooms, a living area, and a bathroom. At around forty square metres, they're considerably bigger than the original ones. But they're put to shame by some of their neighbours' big, modern houses that wouldn't look out of place on my parents' street.

'Those have been built by the wealthier black people who can afford it,' my mother says. 'Rather than move to town, where they might only be able to afford a one-bedroom flat, they stay in the township and build these mansions.'

I wonder how the people in the RDP houses feel about their flashy neighbours.

My mother points out a cluster of simple houses between some trees. 'That's Judah Square, the Rastafarian village,' she says. 'There are two white women living there. One of them married a Rasta.'

I'm not as shocked as I might have been had I not heard the story about the white people in Hornlee first.

We carry on driving, past the Dorothy Broster Children's Home. Named after my mother's ex-boss – Child Welfare's late chairman and president – the home was built eight years ago for abused and neglected children, as well as to accommodate the growing numbers of AIDS orphans in the area.

Our tour takes us through new townships with names I don't recognise. Robololo. Qolweni.

'The Q is a click at the back of your mouth,' says my mother, demonstrating.

A memory crackles in my mind like a radio being tuned.

My mother taught me this when I was little. There are three different kinds of clicks in the Xhosa language, depending on the letter: Q, X or Nc. Without realising it at first, I start clicking my tongue against the roof of my mouth, then my cheek, then I flick it against my teeth.

I look out the window at the houses around us. Some of them are impressive, others are desperate. I think back to the squatters in Oupad, the white people in Hornlee.

South Africa is clearly still a country divided. But the divide, it seems, is no longer black and white. Now, people no longer have to live where they're told because their skin is black or brown. They live where they can afford to, whether that's in a shack in a squatter camp, or an RDP house in a township, or a house with a view in Hornlee, a flat in town, or a waterfront mansion on Leisure Isle. The divide has become an economic one.

One of the unfortunate side effects of this new class system among the black community is a new, indiscriminate type of criminal. On the doors and windows of some of the township houses, even the smallest, poorest ones, I've noticed burglar bars.

'Now *that's* something I've never seen before,' I say to my mother.

'*Ja*, they're stealing from each other now,' she says. 'Things have changed. Everyone's scared. Black, white, brown, it affects everyone.'

I'm aware of affirmative action creating a sudden generation of more affluent black South Africans shortly after the end of apartheid. A quick fix after years of educational and economic disadvantage, affirmative action was criticised by many for being just for show; a cardboard wedge under the crooked table of inequality. There were stories of companies' black cleaners suddenly becoming CEOs: faux-figureheads behind executive desks to indicate their company's commitment to redressing its race ratios.

My father was one of many teachers in South Africa who took early retirement to make way for non-white teachers. Not that he did it for political or even altruistic reasons; the new ANC government made it very attractive financially.

But my mother says it's not just the class divide between black South Africans that's causing the black-on-black crime. It's the xenophobia too.

We've come to *Witlokasie* ('White Location'), the last of the townships on our route. I ask my mother why it's called that and she says no one's quite sure. Some people say it's named after white soldiers who stayed at barracks there to recover after being injured in the Second World War. Others say it's named simply after the colour of those barracks, two white buildings that are still standing today, albeit barely. Their walls are crumbling, the white fading away.

Chapter 17

1982

Being a volunteer, Owéna knew little of Child Welfare's day-to-day business. She'd heard that the society had struggled for many years to replace her after she left in 1972. But she wasn't aware that Miss Broster had been looking for a black social worker specifically. Nor did she know that, when Miss Broster failed to find one, she'd got special permission from the Bantu Administration to appoint a white social worker for the black community instead. She didn't know any of this until Miss Broster offered her the job.

Owéna's instinct was to say no. Working at the crèche with Paula, she'd picked up only the most basic Xhosa words like *Molo* (hello), *Unjani* (how are you?) and *Enkosi Kakhulu* (thank you very much). She felt that the black people deserved someone who could deal with their problems in their own language. Owéna also knew little of the Xhosa culture, which would make it difficult to win the people's trust. And whereas taking her daughter to a crèche was one thing, she could hardly take her along to a shack where a drunk father was abusing his wife and children.

But, having seen the conditions in which the people lived, she also knew that something had to be done.

Owéna spoke to Theron, her mother and her sister. Theron was practical: they could do with the money and if she was going to go up to the squatter camps anyway, she might as well get paid for it. Owéna's mother was distraught: no woman should go back to work after having children, at least not until after they left the house. Owéna's sister, who'd lived in Northern Rhodesia when the trouble started there, was supportive but cautious: who would look after the children if anything happened to her?

Owéna thought it over. The boys were at school and her daughter, at four, was old enough to go to nursery school. Her mother, a housewife, had always been old-fashioned in her views. And having worked at the crèche for a few months, Owéna thought the squatter camps seemed perfectly safe.

The crèche had also given Owéna a chance to get to know the people and their culture better. And it was rewarding to see what effect the crèche was having on the children and their families. Imagine if she could extend that kind of work to the rest of the community. She still didn't speak Xhosa, but she was sure there'd be some kind of book she could buy to help her learn; maybe some cassette tapes.

What it came down to in the end was that she really wanted to do it. It would be a challenge. An adventure. And so, in August 1982, Owéna Schutte went back to work at Child Welfare as the first ever social worker for the black community.

Owéna's first challenge was to help the people help themselves. She knew most black people wouldn't trust her, or even listen to her; they would only listen to their own people who they knew and respected. She also knew from her training that it wasn't a social worker's place to tell a community which issues to prioritise – they had to decide that for themselves.

So she needed the black community to appoint their own committee to represent the people. The committee would identify the problems the people faced, initiate projects that the community could get involved in and be responsible for raising funds to get the projects off the ground. It would also become the sub-committee that Child Welfare needed, by law, to be able to work in the black community in the first place.

The word was put out in the squatter camps that Child Welfare was looking for community representatives. Owéna sent messages to the churches in the squatter camps and placed ads in the local classifieds paper. One by one, the people came forward.

There were church leaders, shop owners and school-teachers; men and women who had both influence and respect in the community. Sometimes they came of their own accord, other times they were nominated by the people.

To cover all the widespread squatter camps, Owéna formed two committees: the Thembalethu committee to represent Flenterlokasie, Witlokasie and Jood-se-Kamp in the west, and Vulindlela to represent Nekkies and Dam-se-Bos in the east.

With the committees in place, Owéna ran monthly meetings where they could put forward the issues they wanted to address. The meetings were usually held in church buildings in the squatter camps, but even when they weren't, each one was opened and closed with a prayer and a hymn.

Now that they had someone to speak to, the people had a lot to say. As a result, the committee meetings could run on for hours. When they started taking place in the evening, Theron put his foot down. He didn't mind his wife working in the squatter camps, but he didn't want her going up there at all hours of the night.

On the condition that Theron would look after the children, Owéna moved the meetings to Sunday afternoons.

From the start, the committees agreed that the children in their community were their number one priority. In particular, they were concerned about the younger children. The Flenterlokasie crèche had shown how valuable a pre-school education was. Now the people wanted to give every child the same opportunity. But the crèche was already full and, even if it could take more children, it was too far out of the way for many. The older children weren't much better off. There was only one primary school, Tembelitsha, serving the entire black community.

Built by the people themselves with what meagre materials they had, the Tembelitsha School was in a dire condition. There were no floors, no ceilings, no electricity and no toilets. The children had no books to learn from, and no books to write in. The few black teachers they managed to find usually didn't stay very long. And the children would only turn up on some days, other days not.

The general living conditions in the squatter camps also came up in every meeting. People had to walk far to get water, and those who got their drinking water from streams were getting sick.

Once she knew what the issues were, Owéna made sure the right people heard about them. Black mothers were approached about starting new crèches. The Knysna Women's

Association and Round Table gave money to build toilets at the Tembelitsha School. The municipality installed water tanks, which they filled regularly with thousands of litres of water.

Often those improvements came as a result of meetings between the black committees and Knysna's town clerk, whose job it was to manage the area's infrastructure and resources. For the first time, there was a dialogue between the black people and the local authorities. The people saw that it was good to talk, and that there were white people willing to listen to them. For Owéna, that was the whole point of her work: to give the people what they needed to help their own community, until the day they didn't need her any more.

Despite her sister in Cape Town constantly telling her she should be careful, Owéna never thought about being scared. Not until she was asked the question outright.

It was a Sunday evening after a committee meeting had typically overrun, and Owéna was getting ready to go home. Outside the Red Church, a man she'd never seen before stopped her. His eyes were the colour of ink.

Wasn't she scared to be there? asked the man.

Owéna met his gaze. No, she said. She wasn't. Her God was with her.

The man simply nodded and walked away. And Owéna realised it was true. She wasn't scared.

Chapter 18

Mrs Burger

Every night before my mother leaves work – and it usually is night by the time she leaves – she calls my father to let him know she's on her way.

When she gets home, there he is, waiting for her at the open kitchen door with the security light on to make sure she gets in safely from the car. The walk is less than ten metres.

My parents' nightly ritual is a new thing; I've never known them to be so cautious before. On the contrary; I remember a time when my parents happily left the doors open during the day and would sometimes forget to lock them at night. Even now, they still don't have burglar bars or trellis doors like everyone else on the street.

Their caution sparks my paranoia. When I lived in Durban ten years ago, I wouldn't think twice about driving home after a night out and walking from the car to the house. Now, I hear my heart with every step of the short walk to my parents' kitchen door. In the dark, the overgrown hibiscus tree between the car and the house suddenly becomes a hiding place for a would-be-rapist. The security light only creates more shadows that make me jump when they move.

It might be that I'm more used to being here in the summer when the days are longer. Or that I've felt safer on previous trips when my brothers and my husband have been here with me. More likely it's the stories I've been hearing and the headlines I've been reading since I got here. A friend of my mother's was recently robbed and assaulted in her home just a few blocks from my parents' house. It was eleven o'clock on a Sunday morning. She was coming home from church.

Handbags are regularly grabbed on busy, sunlit streets. People are raped, even murdered.

At least in Knysna, unlike the rest of the country, every murder still makes the front page of the paper.

None more so than the murder of Dorothy Burger.

At the Knysna library, I find a whole file on Dorothy in a section devoted to noteworthy residents of Knysna. Included in the file are several articles written about her before and after her death. I find out that Mrs Burger was strangled in her home on a Friday afternoon in May 1993. She was eighty-four.

The various tributes that appeared in the local paper remember her as an elegant socialite and a generous host. My mother has told me stories of Dorothy's lavish dinner parties, which were always attended by the who's who of Knysna. She and my father were sometimes invited too, though my mother says they felt terribly out of place as they dined alongside the magistrate and the mayor, the chairman of some or other society and the president of another.

But what made Dorothy Burger's murder so exceptionally

shocking was not her popularity among Knysna's elite; it was her popularity among the coloured and black communities. A tireless campaigner for social welfare, Mrs Burger was a familiar face in all the townships around Knysna.

One article in the file calls her 'no society do-gooder, but a woman deeply committed to serving the needs of the underprivileged'. Another says that she had done so much for the coloured people of Hornlee that the community felt like it had lost one of its own when she died.

What everyone comments on is how generous she always was with her praise and her thanks.

A feature written three years before her death now reads more like an epitaph:

Perhaps the thing for which Mrs Burger – and there is about her a certain graciousness that makes modern first-name informality seem somewhat brash – will be best remembered is her habit of never forgetting a note of appreciation or congratulation or a word of good cheer to those who need it.

Also in the file is a fragile-looking document typed in uneven shades of black on eight onionskin leaves of typing paper. The heading on the first page is 'My trip into wasteland' and I'm startled to read my mother's name in the opening line.

I shall be most grateful if a letter of thanks be sent to Mrs Schutte. Without her help (sometimes physical), I could never have undertaken and hopefully complete this survey.

I skim-read the pages and realise it's a report that Mrs Burger wrote after a series of visits to the squatter camps with my mother, more than twenty-five years ago.

With the report is a hand-written note from Gillian Carter, then head librarian and a regular journalist for the local paper:

This is an amazing document and must be preserved. It gives a first-rate indication of life in the township area in the 80s and 90s. (Mrs Burger herself took me there, she in high heels and immaculate – and loved by everyone be they snotty-nosed children, drink-soaked men or normal folk going about their daily business.)

Mrs Burger was murdered in an unsolved crime which robbed Knysna of a flamboyant, cultured and deeply caring person who really did work amazingly hard for the community. An attitude of paternalism which was part of her own heritage in no way interfered with her total dedication to social welfare. Her sense of humour and her extravagant style give life to this stark picture of shanty life.

I take Gillian's note and the report to the current librarian to be photocopied, handing it over as carefully as though it were the Rosetta Stone.

While I wait, I read over the articles again.

That Dorothy Burger's attacker might have been someone she knew is unthinkable. Yet the articles say there was no sign of forced entry, indicating that either she'd opened the door to the murderer, or he'd had a key to the house.

It makes me sad and scared, not for myself, but for my parents. It seems not even the memories of a person's kindness are enough to protect them any more.

Chapter 19

1983

Owéna knew Dorothy Burger long before they started going to the squatter camps together. A stately woman who was born Afrikaans but had all the grace of an English royal, Mrs Burger was the wife of an ex-principal at Knysna High School, where Theron taught, and a sometime teacher there herself.

Over the years, Owéna and Mrs Burger ran into each other not only at the school, but also at the many events that Mrs Burger hosted, presented, chaired or presided over in some form or another. Founder of the local museum, president of the Arts Society, chairman of the Music Society, divisional commissioner for the Girl Guides and local chairman of the South African National Tuberculosis Association were just some of her titles. She had even been mayor of Knysna for a year.

It was as vice-chairman of the Ladies Benevolent Society that Mrs Burger ended up working alongside Owéna in 1983.

The oldest of Knysna's charitable societies, the Ladies Benevolent Society was founded in the late 1800s, not long after the town itself was founded in 1871, to help the sick and the aged.

Initially the Society worked only among the white community at a time when tuberculosis was rife, but by the 1940s it was addressing the needs of non-whites too. Its objectives at the time included 'providing a supplementary pension to native men (non-drinkers) and 2.6d per month for the land whereon their hut is situated'.

By the 1980s, almost all of the Ladies Benevolent Society's beneficiaries were black; usually people who were waiting for state pensions or disability grants. Those could take months, even years, to process once an application was made, leaving many people with no income during that time.

To help those people survive until their pensions or grants came through, the Ladies Benevolent Society provided them with free food parcels, vouchers for groceries and, in winter, blankets at a minimal cost.

The Society worked closely with Child Welfare and Owéna in particular. As social worker for the black community, she often referred sick and elderly people to the Society for assistance, and advised it on which people genuinely deserved its support.

It took a strong case to persuade the Ladies Benevolent Society to step in, as they could only afford to help forty people with food vouchers every month. But as Knysna's squatter camps grew, so did the number of cases being referred.

To make sure its limited funds were going to those most in need, the Society decided in 1983 to send one of its members into the squatter camps to investigate the health and living conditions of the people it was helping. Dorothy Burger was chosen as the Society's representative. And Owéna was to be her guide.

When Owéna turned up to collect her, Mrs Burger was dressed as immaculately as if she were about to present a

Best Dressed award (an accolade for which Mrs Burger herself had once been runner-up). Her high heels, seamed stockings, neat skirt and rouged lips hardly seemed appropriate for a trip to the squatter camps. But Owéna, dressed in more sensible trousers and flats, said nothing.

When they got to the squatter camps, Mrs Burger was soon praying for her life in the passenger seat of the Child Welfare bakkie, or 'ET' as she would come to call it, short for 'extra terrible'.

As she wrote in her report that night, they:

> bucketed, slithered, slid, groaned and creaked over the most appalling roads, in and out of dongas, and eventually on foot. I buckled myself in securely, locked the door, clung to the handle and with both feet braced, waited for the End. We survived! Below us was spread this beautiful undulating countryside scarred and bled by poverty. Every tin shanty a patchwork quilt of old corrugated iron sheets painted in the favourite colours of their previous owners and now faded into pleasing mellow shades. Picturesque from afar, maybe, but each 'home' a tale of want and hardship.

Over the weeks and months that followed, there were several more visits. Mrs Burger's outfits became no more practical, her reports no less eloquent or evocative. 'Poverty in the raw and filth round and about indescribable,' she wrote about Jood-se-Kamp. 'The road needs expert driving, high-powered ingenuity and full-blooded faith in your maker,' she said of Nekkies. And her verdict on Flenterlokasie: 'The smell of pigs is enough to chloroform any drunk unfortunate enough to fall down and sleep off the effects of the liquor'.

While Owéna had become used to those scenes, Dorothy Burger was witnessing for the first time how the other half lived just over the hill.

Witlokasie, especially, drove it home for her:

> I thought I had seen the worst but such filth . . . can only be believed if witnessed. In some places the wastepaper was so thick that we walked on paper paths . . . and the whole atmosphere was pervaded by the aroma of pig. I could not believe that there were so many extensions of this location I knew nothing of. I was overcome by the rickety houses, some affording no shelter from the stormy blasts and rain, some rooms lying on their sides and everywhere devastating poverty. Yet we were always met with a smile and a little joke . . . a happy lot wallowing in their filth and poverty.

Everywhere they went children followed, their curiosity piqued by the two white women, the one in her flat shoes, the other in her adamant stilettos. Occasionally Owéna led the children in a sing-along, a chorus of small voices singing *Umzi Watsha* (house is burning) or reciting *i-teapoti* (I'm a little teapot), all of them knowing the words and the movements as they dipped their handles and tipped their spouts.

Despite the light relief provided by the children, getting to all of the Society's beneficiaries was an arduous task. With no street names, house numbers or, indeed, roads in the squatter camps, people were difficult to locate. To make it even harder, they usually went by two different names – one English, one Xhosa – and Owéna and Mrs Burger usually had only one or the other name on their list.

When they eventually did find the right shack, Mrs Burger noted down the person's state of health, their living conditions and anything else that struck her as noteworthy to include in her report.

Of one shack, she wrote that the living area was 'just a bare room with absolutely nothing except a tall tin in the middle of the floor, presumably for a fire.' One woman she described as 'a hundred percent disabled, everything the matter with her'. Another woman was mentioned not for her health but for her bosom, which Mrs Burger described as 'unbelievable when not tied up . . . I thought she had stuffed herself with cushions and a couple of pumpkins'.

Mrs Burger's notes were full of stories and anecdotes: how a toothless woman was saving her dentures only for special occasions; how another was half-naked when they got there, getting dressed with her front door open to let the light in because she was almost blind.

On the way home after their last visit, Mrs Burger asked Owéna how she did it: how she went to those squatter camps every day and didn't go home weeping every night.

She couldn't let it get to her, Owéna explained. If she did, she wouldn't be able to help them.

That night Dorothy Burger finished her report, writing of a man named Jackson:

He sits there on that dingy bed covered with filthy grey blankets, no sheets in a room bereft of every thought of comfort or seating accommodation except that awful bed. I can weep . . . curse . . . bring the world about my ears to see him helpless in such abject poverty and he smiles and says 'Dit gaan baie goed.'

It's going very well.

Chapter 20

Crèche tour

I'm getting another tour of the townships, but this time it isn't my mother taking me. I'm going with Lesley Satchel, my nursery school teacher from when I was five years old.

Lesley was the head teacher at Stepping Stones, the nursery school where she taught me, and my brothers before me. I find our class picture in my photo album, a happy group of white boys and girls sitting in and around a tree. Our faces are frozen in wide smiles, several of them with missing front teeth. Standing next to us are Lesley and her teaching assistant Denise, whose face is the only brown one in the photo.

Lesley is retired from teaching now, but she's still involved with education in various guises. As a trustee of the Knysna Education Trust, she's especially involved in the many crèches and day-care centres that are now dotted around Knysna's townships and squatter camps.

The first crèche we go to is named after Paula Witney, my mother's ex-colleague from Child Welfare. I met Paula for a coffee recently and she said this is the only crèche she's still involved with – not, she hastened to add, because it's named after her, but because it's the one in most need.

The crèche does look run-down. In the playground, two broken swings have been flung over their wooden frame. Inside the building there are no curtains on the windows and there's little to look at on the walls, except for a few laminated posters of lions, elephants, buffalo, leopards and rhinos: Africa's Big Five.

Still, it's considerably better than the crèches my mother took me along to when I was little. For a start, there are tables and chairs in the classrooms, and in the playground there's a big jungle gym resembling a boat that puts even the one I remember at Stepping Stones to shame. Lesley tells me it was a donation from the Naval Cadets, who come to town every year as part of the Oyster Festival.

We're not the only visitors here today. A tour group of five white women and one white man is huddled together in the playground taking pictures of the children, who are putting on a little show. A nursery rhyme in Xhosa – about a cow with horns and a tail, from what I can tell from the accompanying actions – is followed by an especially speedy rendition of the South African national anthem, *Nkosi Sikelel' iAfrika*. Introduced in 1994 by new president Nelson Mandela, the anthem combines lyrics in Xhosa, Zulu and Sesotho in the first two verses, while the last two verses are based on the national anthem I grew up with, *Die Stem* ('The Voice'), in Afrikaans and English.

'Let us live and strive for freedom, in South Aaaafrica . . . our . . . laaaaand!' The children draw out the last word until it becomes a cheer. The tourists clap and coo and hand the children sweets from a plastic bag that the black tour guide passes round. Next to me, Lesley mumbles disapprovingly, something about junk food and mixed messages.

There are two classrooms inside the building, one for Grade R, or 'reception', where six year olds are prepared for 'big school', and the other for the five year olds in the year below.

I'm impressed by the daily programme on a neatly written poster on the wall, which includes things like 'creative activities' and 'story-time' for the younger kids and 'mental maths' and 'educational games' for the older ones. The programme also includes breakfast, a mid-morning snack and lunch. Next door there's a kitchen where big pots of food are being prepared.

For breakfast, Lesley tells me, the children get ePap, the brand-name for an enriched maize porridge that's distributed to all the crèches in the area. For lunch, they get a cooked meal.

When it's time to go, a small crowd of children gathers around us to say goodbye. One boy wants to see my camcorder and is fascinated when he can see his friends on the small screen. He waves his hand behind the flip-out screen and looks disappointed when it doesn't come up in the picture. I show him how it's done, waving my own hand in front of the lens. Before long, I'm surrounded by children shoving each other to get a look, until I'm almost pushed over and have to fight my way out like Gulliver against the Lilliputians.

It brings back a memory of four-year-old me surrounded by a similar group of black children when I was visiting a crèche with my mother. Except all they wanted to do then was touch my blonde hair.

We leave at the same time as the tour group, who are

discussing the crèche on their way out. 'They're so happy, aren't they?' says one of the ladies in what I'm surprised to hear is not a British or a German or an American accent, but a South African one.

On the way to the next crèche, Lesley and I compare what we've seen with the squatter-camp crèches of twenty-six years ago.

'Oh, it's like chalk and cheese,' says Lesley.

She tells me that all the crèche teachers are now getting proper training, and what a difference it's made. But there's still work to be done.

'I know it's bad, but it's *so* much better than it was,' says Lesley. 'And it can't get better without going through all the stages of improvement. But it's on its way.'

We arrive at Ethembeni, the only crèche that's left from my mother's days.

Ethembeni was one of the last crèches to start up during my mother's time at Child Welfare – in August 1988, according to a sign on the side of the building. It was also the first with its own premises built from scratch at a time when most crèches and playgroups were held in dilapidated church buildings.

My mother has a framed picture of Ethembeni in her office at Epilepsy South Africa. In it, a small group of children stand proudly in front of the new-looking building.

Lesley tells me that finding or funding buildings is the main problem for crèches. Some people try to start playgroups in their own homes but the government won't give them any money towards it if it's on private property. She can see the government's reasoning, though.

'You can't just think, "Oh, I'm going to improve my house and make a preschool here and then someone will come and build me an extra toilet or something",' says Lesley. 'Because you'd have everybody in the township having a preschool for two years just to get their property upgraded.'

Lesley is fiddling with a gate to get us in. The fence around Ethembeni is topped with scary-looking razor wire and there are burglar bars on the windows.

A stripy awning over the front door makes the crèche a bit more inviting.

Once we're in, Lesley points out a vegetable garden that runs along one side of the fence. It's just a thin strip of dry-looking ground but a few spinach leaves are coming up.

'This has gone on for years, this little veggie garden here,' says Lesley. 'It's little, but it's there.'

She knocks on a side door where a woman called Agnes greets her. Agnes looks a little apprehensive when she sees my camcorder, but when she hears I'm Nobantu's daughter, she smiles.

'I saw you at Queenie's funeral,' she says.

She agrees to show us around.

There's a pleasant smell of food cooking when we walk into the main building. About thirty children – all four years old, Agnes tells us – are sitting at yellow and red and blue and green plastic tables on equally colourful plastic chairs. Some of them don't even look up from the puzzles they're building, others stare at me and Lesley with big eyes. The room is big and busy. On one wall, there's a mural of a tree painted in primary colours. A 'house corner' has a wooden toy stove and a desk with a phone. In a 'make-believe area', there's a small pile of dress-up clothes.

The room next door is much noisier. 'These are the two and three year olds,' says Agnes, having to raise her voice. A few of the children are huddling by the doorway where toys and dolls are scattered on the floor. One boy is waving around a naked white baby doll with blonde hair. A girl next to him chews on a dirty teddy bear's ear.

The teacher gathers the children on the carpet to sing for us. I recognise the tunes but the words are new. To the tune of 'Frère Jacques', they sing: 'I am growing, yum yum ePap, look at me, look at me, I'm a little flower, I'm a little flower, ePap helps, look at me.'

Lesley stands among the children, singing along as she picks up the words.

Next they sing a rousing chorus of 'London's Burning', only they've changed it to 'House is burning' and sing it not only in English but also in Xhosa and Afrikaans.

After the song, Lesley tries to explain to the children that they've been singing 'London's Burning' and that I come from London. They just look at her blankly.

Next Agnes shows us the baby room, the latest addition to Ethembeni. It's nap time and about twenty tiny children are sleeping on their stomachs on thin sponge mattresses on the floor. The youngest babies sleep in white cots lined up along the walls.

Three of those cots were donated by a Swiss exchange student, Lesley says. The girl had been staying with Lesley and her husband for a year, and had been so taken with Ethembeni that she donated the cots and came back with her father when her year was up to complete the baby room.

Around the corner from the baby room is the kitchen, where the delicious smells have been coming from. The cook is dishing up rice from a huge pot. Today the children are having cabbage and carrots and mince with their rice, she says.

Lesley approves. 'Cabbage and carrots are very healthy,'

she says to the cook. 'I think during the war those were the only things they could grow in England and the whole population survived on cabbage and carrots.'

We're back in the room of four year olds, where we're treated to more singing. This time it's Old Mandela, not Old Macdonald, who had a farm, ee-i-ee-i-oh.

The children are having their lunch soon so we start saying our goodbyes. When I reach the door, a boy runs up to me with his hand clenched in a tiny thumbs-up. 'Sharp!' he shouts. I have no idea what he means, except that 'sharp' in South Africa has a similar meaning to 'cool'. Not knowing what else to do, I give him a thumbs-up back. He presses his thumb against mine and flicks it to the side. 'Sharp!' he says again.

Before I know it, I've got ten four year olds at my feet, all of them sticking out their thumbs and calling 'Sharp! Sharp!' I flick their thumbs one by one, feeling like a celebrity in a crowd of autograph-hunters.

The last boy who gets a flick is wearing an orange T-shirt with just one word on it in bright, rounded letters like those alphabet fridge magnets you get for kids.

'Happy', it says.

Chapter 21

1983

When the Flenterlokasie crèche was full to capacity with sixty-five children, Child Welfare opened a second crèche in Jood-se-Kamp. Sixty children turned up on the first day.

Three mornings a week, the toddlers at the crèches played, listened to stories and sang songs. But for Owéna, that wasn't enough. The children needed a more thought-through programme of learning and playing if they were going to develop properly.

Owéna knew she and Paula weren't the best people to give them that development, not only because they weren't qualified, but because they were no longer involved in the day-to-day running of the crèches. For that they now had volunteers from the black community. The 'crèche mamas', as the children called them, were mothers and grandmothers themselves and entirely committed to their new roles. But they didn't have any training either. Many of them had never even gone to school.

Owéna had a plan.

137

For the People

The next time she picked up her daughter from nursery school, she asked Lesley Satchel, the head-teacher, for help.

Stepping Stones had four classrooms with educational toys and posters and paints and brushes and everything else pre-schoolers needed to learn and develop. They also had four qualified nursery teachers and another four assistants.

A young woman with an open mind, Lesley agreed right away when Owéna asked for help training the crèche mamas.

If Owéna could bring the crèche mamas down to Stepping Stones once a month, Lesley said she and her team would happily put together a training programme for them.

When Owéna turned up on the first day with twelve women and a Xhosa interpreter, Lesley and her team had the afternoon all planned out. Starting with the theme of 'my body', they would show the crèche mamas how to run a simple exercise.

A typical example of so-called 'integrated learning', the exercise involved cutting out a face from a magazine, gluing it onto a page and drawing in the rest of the body. In 'real life', once a class had done that, the teachers would usually tell them a story or teach them a rhyme that would help the children remember the new words they'd learned.

The aim of the exercise, as the Stepping Stones teachers explained to the crèche mamas, was to start giving children the skills they needed to learn to read and write. The cutting, gluing and drawing helped to develop their fine motor skills and hand-eye coordination. The stories and rhymes helped to develop their vocabulary. And by using different types of paper, card, pens, pencils and crayons, the children got a feel for the different tools they could use to write.

To move things along, the Stepping Stones teachers had

some ready-made examples where they'd already cut out and stuck down the faces and drawn in the bodies. But they soon saw that the crèche mamas were struggling to understand the instructions. The teachers realised they'd have to take a step back, and let the crèche mamas do the exercise themselves.

Half an hour later, the crèche mamas were still trying to cut out faces, their own faces screwed-up in concentration and their fingers shaky on the plastic handles of the child-friendly scissors. Gluing wasn't much quicker, as the women struggled to grip the thick brushes. Because of poor schooling and, in some cases, no schooling at all, the crèche mamas' own fine motor skills were completely undeveloped.

Books were also alien to them. The Xhosa people had a rich storytelling tradition, but it was an oral one. So when faced with a physical book, the crèche mamas didn't know what to do with it. The language barrier didn't help either. All the books at Stepping Stones were in English and Afrikaans, and although a few Xhosa children's books existed, they weren't available in Knysna. The best the teachers could do was try to explain the principle of written books and stories to the crèche mamas, and hope they would go away and make their own books and posters with what few materials they had.

That was, if the crèche mamas even understood what they'd learned in the first place. Xhosa interpreters liked to add their own flavour to their translations, which could lead to much confusion and misinterpretation. And the women, being illiterate, were unable to take notes.

Despite the gaps in communication, the crèche mamas were impressed with what they saw. And they wanted it all: the colourful posters and the climbing frames and the boxes full of wool and lace and buttons and hessian for the children to make things with.

Hearing how the crèche mamas compared Stepping Stones with their own crèches, Owéna explained to them how hard the white parents worked to make and keep Stepping Stones that way. She would know – she was one of the mothers who baked cakes and biscuits by the car-boot-load for fundraising cake sales. Fathers painted classrooms and made jungle gyms and helped to fix leaky roofs and broken equipment. And almost all the materials the children used for their arts and crafts, from off-cuts of fabric to old magazines, were collected and donated by the parents. The crèche mamas were amazed. Their own people would never do that, they said.

If the black community wasn't willing or able to help the crèches, there were plenty of other people who were. Tuberculosis charity SANTA gave fortified biscuits and milk that the children drank out of empty yoghurt cups donated by the public. Knysna businesses gave reams of used computer paper printed only on one side, leaving the other side blank for drawing and painting. Appeals to the public brought in crayons, pencils, magazines, colouring-in books, building blocks, balls and toys.

Bit by bit, the crèche mamas started applying what they were learning at Stepping Stones. Before long, each crèche had a 'house corner' where girls could play with toy pots, pans and measuring spoons. There they would 'cook' for dolls and teddy bears, which they tied to their backs like babies, just as their mothers had done with them.

The crèche mamas showed the children how to cut things and glue them down, paint shapes with powder paint and identify the colours they were using – not always easy, as the word for blue and green was the same in Xhosa until the new Xhosa word *iBlou*, from the Afrikaans for blue, was eventually coined.

The children learned to write their names: 'Gloria', 'Pauline', 'Grace'. At first the crèche mamas wrote the names for the children to copy, as they'd been shown at Stepping Stones. But it wasn't long before the children could write their own from memory.

The difference in the children was soon noticed not only by their parents, but by the rest of their community too.

In the spring of 1983, Owéna was approached by a black woman called Mam Tau.

Mrs Tau was called 'Mam' because she was a schoolteacher or 'madam'. She had her own small school in Dam-se-Bos that she opened when she saw how far the children had to walk to Tembelitsha – a dangerous route where gangs of young men often assaulted children and raped women. Worried about the children, she started her school specifically for the youngest ones of six and seven years old.

By the time Mam Tau came to Owéna, she had forty children packed into a tiny church in Dam-se-Bos where she tried to teach them. But it was difficult when the children had not even the most basic of skills. Most of the children didn't even know how to hold a pencil when they came to her school. They'd never had an opportunity to try; their parents simply didn't have the money to buy them paper and crayons.

Mam Tau herself barely had enough money to buy basic supplies for the school, so to preserve her paper and pencils, she taught the children to draw and write with sticks in the dirt outside.

But it couldn't go on like that, and that was why Mam

Tau came to Owéna. Dam-se-Bos desperately needed a crèche, she said. Like the ones in Flenterlokasie and Jood-se-Kamp.

Owéna had no difficulty finding volunteer crèche mamas to help. The Dam-se-Bos crèche opened that summer, followed swiftly by another in the squatter camp that would become known as Oupad, where Queenie lived.

Queenie, who had always loved being around children, volunteered to help at the Oupad crèche. She had a day a week that she wasn't working, and was happy to give it up to become a crèche mama. With four crèches up and running, almost two hundred black preschool children were able to learn and play every week.

But the crèches were still in the squatter camps. And despite those squatter camps being just outside Knysna with its lagoon and its beaches, for many children the most water they'd ever seen was the stream in which they washed. Some of them had never left the squatter camps at all, not even to go down into town.

When Owéna realised this, she decided to take the children to the beach. Every child, she thought, should get the chance to play in the sea.

In 1983, however, that was easier said than done.

Owéna and Theron usually took their own children swimming at Buffalo Bay, a four-kilometre stretch of white sand with a sizeable swimming area watched by a lifeguard. But Buffalo Bay was more than twenty kilometres from Knysna. And even if Owéna could get the crèche children there, they wouldn't be able to get near that four-kilometre beach. They wouldn't even get close enough to see the car park where the dune buggies and the Volkswagen Kombis spilled white families and their sun umbrellas onto the sandy Tarmac.

That was because they'd have to stop well before the car park. Not because of the Stop sign telling them to, but because of the tiny plaque under the Stop sign that said 'Whites Only'.

The sign indicated the furthest point that anyone black or coloured could go, unless they worked in the Buffalo Bay caravan park, or the cafe, or in any one of the several white-owned holiday homes in the area. Any other coloured or black people who wanted to go swimming at Buffalo Bay had to go to the beach for non-whites, a small patch of sand surrounded by rocks and a violent sea with dangerous currents. Owéna couldn't take the children there.

Much nearer to Knysna town, there were other, smaller beaches at the Heads and Leisure Island, but it was generally accepted that those, like the main beach at Buffalo Bay, were for whites only. Generally accepted, but not spelled out.

That was good enough for Owéna.

She investigated the options. The Heads wouldn't do, as the sea was too rough for small children. Bollard Bay on Leisure Island was no good either, as it had only a thin strip of beach when the tide was out. But around the corner from Bollard Bay was the Green Hole, a natural pond with a grassy picnic area complete with toilets and built-in stands for *braais*, South Africans' beloved barbecues. Theron warned Owéna that she couldn't take the children there. There could be trouble, he said.

But Owéna was determined, and he let her be.

With the parents' permission, Owéna and the crèche mamas loaded Child Welfare's bakkie and a few minibuses full of children and took them to the Green Hole.

At first, the children had mixed reactions. Some of them

were out of their clothes and in the water straight away. Others stood back, scared of the brown water that got almost black towards the middle. But even those who never made it into the water were soon playing on the sand.

It wasn't long before the police arrived.

The yellow van drove past once, twice before parking next to the Child Welfare bakkie. Two policemen walked straight up to Owéna, ignoring the crèche mamas.

The children couldn't be there, they said. The residents of Leisure Island had complained.

Owéna didn't care about the residents, and she told the police so. But she did care about the children, she said, and the Green Hole was the only safe place for them to swim. If the police thought she was going to watch a child drown because some residents couldn't handle having some four year olds on their beach, they had another thing coming.

The policemen saw it was pointless arguing with Owéna, and with a muttered threat of coming back if there was any trouble, they were on their way.

They never did come back, not that day.

On the way back to Flenterlokasie, Owéna had a bakkie full of children under the canopy in the back and two crèche mamas with her in the front. The children were singing, no doubt sugar-buzzing from the sweets they were given at the end of the day; little individual bags of penny sweets that Owéna and the volunteers had packed and tied with brightly coloured wool.

Just before they got to the squatter camp, one of the crèche mamas turned to Owéna and said something that would stay with her for the rest of her life.

'I hope that one day, before these children pick up a stone

to throw at a white man, they remember what you did for them today.'

Owéna took all of the crèche children to the Green Hole at least once after that day. The first few times the police turned up again, just driving past slowly, watching. But eventually they stopped coming altogether.

Meanwhile, articles about the crèches in the local paper were drawing interest from people in the Knysna area, including those who worked in the town's growing tourist industry. One particularly popular tourist day out was a ferry ride on the lagoon to Featherbed Bay, a nature reserve on the western of the two Heads. Once there, holidaymakers were taken on a hike through the reserve where they could explore the natural caves and spot the rare butterflies and endangered antelope. The day would usually end with lunch in a pretty restaurant under a canopy of trees, before the tourists were ferried back to their luxury cars and their tour buses.

Outside the holiday season, however, the ferry was moored on the side of the lagoon more often than not. Reading about the black crèches in the *Herald*, the married couple who ran the trips spotted an opportunity.

They offered to take the children on the ferry, for free.

More than just a ferry ride, the children got a whole day out at Featherbed Bay. And although it didn't include the hike or the fancy lunch that the tourists paid top dollar, pound and deutschmark for, the children were allowed to play on the beach, swim in the sea and eat sandwiches in the restaurant under the trees. For many of them, though, the ferry ride itself was the highlight, as they had never been on a boat.

Next came a call from a group of retired engineers who had built a miniature railway in the Knysna hills, where model steam engines pulled sit-on carriages along a circuit through a pretty piece of woodland. They wanted to offer the crèche children free rides on the trains.

The scale of the trains didn't matter to the crèche children. All that mattered was that they were going on a train. Some of them believed they were going all the way to Cape Town, a city they had only ever heard of. Many of them turned up in pretty dresses and shiny shoes, their parents having dressed them in their Sunday best for the occasion.

When the train didn't take them to Cape Town, the children didn't seem to mind. They still went home with stories of the steam engine with its whistle that went toot-toot.

For some of those children, the ones in the squatter camp that would become known as Oupad, it would be their last happy memory for a while.

Chapter 22

1983

Owéna wasn't against the new highway. The road would actually be a welcome relief, as the narrow stretch of N2 coming over the hill into Knysna was dangerous and the traffic often got backed up behind big trucks. But as soon as she heard that black families would have to be moved to make way for the road, it became her problem. And when she saw where they were going to be moved to, that problem became a battle.

By the time Owéna heard about the temporary township, it was already being built, out of sight of the squatter camps where she'd been working. If Owéna had been angry about the Leisure Island residents complaining about her crèche children on their beach, it was nothing compared with her reaction to the sight that met her in the temporary township.

On a crudely terraced slope between Dam-se-Bos and Jood-se-Kamp, rows of pastel yellow and pink and blue and green boxes, little bigger than shipping containers, were being packed in next to each other.

The walls were made of hardboard, nailed to a thin wooden frame with a cheap tin roof. Below the roof there was no ceiling, below that no floor, just the bare ground that was already getting muddy from a recent downpour. There was no chimney either, making it dangerous for families to use their wood-burning stoves. And although bucket toilets were a step up from the pit toilets the people of Oupad were used to, they now had to share those toilets with their neighbours.

The authorities insisted that the houses were meant to last for just six months, while the official black township was being built. But Owéna couldn't see them lasting even that long.

As a final insult, the temporary township was to be called 'Bongani', Xhosa for 'Praise the Lord'.

It was Owéna's job to look out for the black community's welfare. But this was more personal than that. Because one of the families that would have to move was Queenie's.

On Owéna's next trip to Bongani, she took along Gillian Carter to write an exposé for the local paper.

Gillian was as appalled as Owéna when she saw the flimsy houses that the people of Oupad were being moved to. The thin hardboard walls were already warping from the sun and rain, and the roofs sagged in the middle.

Later that week, Gillian's article appeared in the *Knysna-Plett Herald* under the headline 'Black pawns in shock move'. In her closing paragraph, she wrote:

> I spoke to a number of black people affected by this move. And all of them said it would be impossible to live in the temporary houses. But the question remains – what option do they have?

Gillian's article caused a stir with the public and the authorities. With their project now under the spotlight, the provincial government and the local municipality agreed to make at least some improvements to the Bongani houses.

In an attempt to counteract the bad PR, the municipality didn't waste any time. Services were fast-tracked: when the official tender process for water tanks took too long, a plumber was simply asked to phone around for quotes and the cheapest tanks were bought. Houses were lifted on one side, so that the roofs would be at enough of an angle for rainwater to run down them. The mud floors were filled in and compacted. And when the higher floors meant the doors could no longer open properly, they were simply sawn down until they did.

Meanwhile, Owéna was putting together a profile of the Oupad families to identify potential welfare issues in the temporary township. With her colleague Vivien to help, she went from door to door noting the details of each family: how many of them there were, how many children, which religious denomination they belonged to, anything that would help to make sure the authorities put the necessary facilities, schools and churches in place.

At meetings between the provincial government and the Knysna Municipality, Owéna and Miss Broster fought the black community's corner. It wasn't that Child Welfare didn't appreciate the temporary houses, Owéna said in one of those meetings. But they had to be fit for human beings. And they weren't, not with their cramped living conditions, the absence of any kind of kitchen, the toilets being right next to the back doors, or the muddy, uneven mess where floors should have been. Owéna doubted that the houses would be very temporary, not when it was going to be at least another two years before the official township was built.

The day the trucks and the bulldozers turned up came as much as a surprise to Owéna as to the people whose houses were being demolished.

She was in the office when she got the news. Ten minutes and several broken speed limits later, she was in Oupad, where she found Queenie standing outside her house watching her furniture being manhandled onto a truck.

The last Owéna had heard before that day, the Oupad families would be given a reasonable time to make any necessary improvements to their new Bongani houses before they'd be expected to move in. But Queenie, for one, had been so unprepared for the move that she had sent her daughter to school that morning, not realising the child wouldn't have a home to come back to.

It wasn't the first time Queenie and Tiny were being moved. Ten years before, theirs had been one of the twenty-two houses that were bulldozed in Hunters Home. When they were taken from Hunters Home to the area that would eventually become known as Oupad, there were already some families living there, coloured as well as black.

After initially building their own, small house near the forest on the edge of the settlement, Queenie and Tiny soon needed more room for their growing family. So when an old lady put her house nearer the road up for sale, Tiny bought it.

Tiny and Queenie gradually extended their new home so it had three bedrooms – one for them, one for their two girls and one for their baby boy – as well as a kitchen, a living room, a dining room and an outhouse with a pit toilet.

They also had a small vegetable garden where they grew carrots and cabbages, and an enclosure where they kept cattle. Next to that, they built a church.

Now, almost ten years later, Queenie could only watch as the house and the church were demolished and the cattle trampled her cabbages.

Despite the municipality's promises to the contrary, Owéna found that the Bongani houses had barely been improved by the time the families moved in.

She heard the stories every Tuesday and Friday when she took Queenie home. During one heavy rainfall, Queenie said so much water had flowed into her house that the children had to stay home from school to help bail it out. They were at it all day in the driving rain, the wet and the cold just as bad inside the house as out.

Rain also caused problems in the Bongani cemetery, which had been created in a hurry on a steep clay slope. With insistent rain eroding the slope, coffins became exposed, sticking out of the earth like broken keys on a piano.

Owéna could only imagine how distressing it must have been for the Xhosa people, most of whom were deeply religious and spiritual.

Like their neighbours, Queenie and Tiny had no choice but to settle in to Bongani as best they could. Using planks and metal salvaged from their old Oupad home, Tiny built extra rooms onto their little house. To cover the damp, rotting walls of the original structure, Queenie wallpapered them with pages from old magazines, and hung net curtains in the windows.

However long they would be there for, the least they could do was try to make it feel like home.

Chapter 23

Oupad

There's one story my mother keeps going back to whenever I ask about her time at Child Welfare. She still gets angry when she talks about it now, about Bongani and the people who were made to move there.

I want to hear the other side of the story, the official side. And I know just the man to ask.

Oom Piet is dismissive when I first bring up Bongani. The people, he says, were squatting in the area where the N2 road had to be widened.

'We had to move them, and we had to accommodate them somewhere. And that was that.'

One of my mother's criticisms has always been that the people were given no notice to move, but Oom Piet tells a different story.

'I gave them notice myself,' he says. 'Walked from house to house, myself.'

But not everyone was home when he went round, he says. So he left messages with neighbours and told people to come to the Bantu Administration office so he could explain to them what was going on.

'If they wanted to know, they would have known,' he says. 'But some people only hear what suits them.'

He was there on the day the people were moved, he says. When I ask him how they reacted, he admits that there were naturally those who were resistant. But as far as he's concerned, they had no right to be.

'If I come to you and say, "Look, they're building a road here. The road is essential. This house will have to come down. But don't worry, we're going to build you a house there." I think it's a fair deal. After all, whose land is that you're living on? It's not yours. You don't have anyone's permission to build your house there.'

Most people got bigger houses in Bongani than they'd had before, says Oom Piet. That's not what I've heard from my mother, or read in Gillian Carter's article in the *Herald*.

Oom Piet's argument is that, although the houses in Oupad might have been bigger, there were often several families living together. Whereas in Bongani, each family got their own house.

I pull out a photo of Bongani shortly after it was built. My mother took it to prove how dire the conditions were when Child Welfare was applying for extra funding to help. In the picture, a tiny house painted pastel yellow is visibly warping.

Oom Piet is unfazed when I point it out, saying the warping happened as time went by. 'All of those houses had to do longer service in the end than was probably originally planned,' he says. 'Because, as you know, the wheels of the state turn slowly.'

He's referring to the development of the official black township. The plan was that Bongani would only be a temporary solution while the proper township was being built, and the houses weren't supposed to last longer than six months.

But it took another seven years for the township to be completed. And some of those hardboard houses in Bongani were still there until very recently.

Oom Piet insists that there are two sides to every story.

'It's easy for an outsider to come in and comment and say things that they don't know anything about,' he says. I don't get the sense that he's referring to me.

'Remember, these were incredibly sensitive issues. You're working with people who have the least. And who have all the obstacles against them. If you didn't physically walk and live and work there, you didn't know how it looked there.'

I think of my mother, who did walk and work there, and whose version of events is very different from his.

Oom Piet looks pensive. He took many 'hits', he says, in big meetings with important people. He starts saying something else, but stops himself.

I press him to tell me what he was going to say.

'It was just a case of . . .' he trails off. He's been very confident throughout our conversation but now he struggles to find the words. 'I always said, the good news, the positive news, they always went and broke themselves. And when it was bad news, I had to go and do it.'

He goes quiet for a moment. 'But that was probably part of the process,' he says.

Chapter 24

Tembelitsha

I've heard it said that there was at least one good thing about Bongani: the school. It was small and only went up to standard two, or grade four, but it meant the children didn't have to walk to Tembelitsha; a journey so far that most of them didn't bother in the colder winter months.

The distance wasn't the only reason the Oupad and Bongani families didn't want their children to go to Tembelitsha. My mother says the school buildings were in an appalling state and there were no facilities to speak of, prompting many parents at the time to send their children away to school in other towns if they could afford it.

Tembelitsha still exists, but it isn't the original school that I've seen in my mother's pictures from the 1980s. It's moved to a different part of Witlokasie, to new premises built especially for the purpose.

I'm curious to see how the new Tembelitsha compares with the old one in the pictures, and arrange to meet the principal. The school isn't far from my mother's office, and she offers to drop me off during her lunch break.

We turn off Witlokasie's gravel road onto a bumpy driveway that leads up to the school, a series of long, single-storey brick buildings with grey metal grates on the windows.

Surrounding Tembelitsha is a fence with barbed wire on top, but it doesn't look terribly secure. Next to the car park there's a small vegetable garden that's covered to protect it from the elements. A cow wanders into the car park and a security guard chases it away.

'This is an AIDS Friendly School' says a hand-painted sign on the side of one building.

I look at the grates on the windows, thinking they must obscure the children's view of the outside world. But it's not the most inspiring view in the first place. Around the school, shacks are packed in next to each other and layabouts in tattered clothes wander among the cows and goats that graze on what little grass there is.

It's a far cry from Knysna Primary, where my brothers and I spent our first school years. Situated in the middle of town, it has a swimming pool and tennis courts and a small rugby field.

Mrs Martin, the acting principal, comes to meet me in reception. The hellos are slightly awkward and I get the sense that I've caught her off-guard; that maybe she's forgotten I was coming.

She sits me down in her office, where we're joined by a colleague of hers, Mr Guga. Like everyone else I've seen at the school, they're both black.

An assistant serves us coffee and I hesitate. I'm not supposed to have caffeine because of migraines, and haven't had a cup of coffee for years. But I don't want to offend Mrs Martin by turning it down. I remember my mother telling me she was once in a similar situation when she was offered a glass of milk during one of her visits to the squatter camps. It was curdled but she drank it anyway, resisting the urge to gag as the lumps slid down her throat. She hasn't had a glass of milk since.

I drink the coffee.

Mr Guga and Mrs Martin paint a dismal picture of life at the township school, where most of the children come from disadvantaged and illiterate homes, often affected in one way or another by AIDS. Their families can't afford to pay school fees, buy books or uniforms or even give them a packed lunch. As a result, the school is classified as the poorest of the poor, which means it's completely subsidised by the government and free to attend. It's one of the main reasons many black families still choose to send their children to Tembelitsha instead of Knysna Primary in town. That, and the fact that Tembelitsha teaches them in Xhosa as well as English.

Despite Tembelitsha's official classification as poor, Mr Guga says the parents think the school has money. Mrs Martin says it's difficult to get parents to help with things like painting classrooms or fixing toilets, because they want to be paid for their efforts. Mr Guga puts it down to the parents being more knowledgeable now about what's going on in the world. They can listen to the government's Budget on the radio or the television and hear how much has been allocated to education.

'But they don't count the chairs, they don't count the books, they don't count the food that is being eaten,' says Mr Guga, referring to the meals that are provided for the children every day as part of a feeding scheme which, according to him, is the best thing that's happened to the school since the ANC came into power.

The problem, says Mrs Martin, is that some parents don't value education. She says it was different in the old days. She's been at Tembelitsha since 1989, when it was her first teaching job. 'That time,' she says, 'the parents, they did care. Because they respected the teacher, they respected education. They were so engaged. Whenever there was something going on, they came to the school, they supported the school. But now, they're less involved. I'm not saying they don't care now. But the level is not the same when I compare it to that time.'

Mr Guga chimes in. 'There are still parents who really love the activities that are happening at the school. There are a number of parents who come in. And now you'll find the parents that are involved are middle-aged. Not like in the olden days where you got the old people. Even if you look at the governing body now, it's . . .'

Mrs Martin completes his sentence: 'It's young guys. Young blood.'

The conversation turns to security, which Mr Guga says is a big issue. Vandalism and burglary are common, and people from the surrounding township often come in to the school to use the toilets or, in some cases, steal the toilet pipes. Even the vegetables in the school garden were stolen during the recent winter break.

Those people don't value education, says Mr Guga. But, he adds, there are some people in the townships who do. People whose children or grandchildren come to school every day and are willing to learn, despite being from broken families where a parent or even both parents have died from AIDS, or their parents are unemployed and have no money for food.

I ask them what they reckon the best thing is about Tembelitsha.

They're quiet for a long time. Mrs Martin laughs, then goes quiet again.

It's Mr Guga who eventually comes up with an answer.

'The very best thing is that we've got committed and dedicated teachers here. Teachers with passion. Committed staff.'

Mrs Martin nods in agreement.

My final question is what 'Tembelitsha' means. They answer simultaneously.

'New hope.'

I have some time before my mother comes to pick me up, and one of the teaching assistants, Victoria Sigcu, offers to give me a tour of the school. She's only too happy to show me around; she loves my mother and doesn't hold back in telling me so.

Back in 1988, Victoria was one of the children at Ethembeni, the last crèche my mother started.

She takes me into several classrooms, all of them with the ugly metal grates on their windows. I've got my camcorder and, on seeing it, the children wave and cheer and pose.

In one classroom there are handmade posters on the wall explaining different types of soil, electricity and fractions. In another class there's a mural of music notes, with illustrated alphabet cards around the edges: K for *ikati*: cat. L for *iloli*: lorry. M for *umama*: mother.

In a computer room there are rows of desktop machines. I wonder how many have been stolen.

In the last classroom we go to, the teacher beckons for the children to stand up. They start singing, their eyes closed. It sounds like some kind of hymn and, although I can't understand the Xhosa words, I find it intensely moving as their young voices break away from each other in beautiful harmonies.

Looking at these children, I can see there really is new hope at Tembelitsha.

Chapter 25

1983

When Owéna first came across Tembelitsha, she thought it must have seen better days – but the older teachers assured her it hadn't been much different when it first opened in 1971. Owéna was shocked when she saw the conditions in which the children were expected to learn. The main school building was just four classrooms made of rotting, untreated wood, with planks so crudely hammered together that the wind whistled through them. A tin roof sat directly on the walls with no ceiling in between, so that drops of condensation dripped on the children in the cold winter months. To help the children stay warm, teachers made fires in empty oil drums in the middle of the classrooms. With few windows and no electricity, the fires also provided much-needed light.

Classroom floors were bare dirt, which had to be scrubbed with manure to create a smooth, compact surface. First thing every morning, the schoolchildren went out to collect the manure from cows in the surrounding squatter camp, then spent their first 'lesson' of the day on their hands and knees rubbing the manure into the floor.

Actual lessons weren't much more educational. There were few textbooks and no exercise books or stationery at all; instead the children wrote on slates with chalk. Those children whose parents couldn't afford to buy them slates had to write in the dirt with sticks.

With limited space in the main school, neighbouring churches had to be used as classrooms. Further away, Mam Tau's school in Dam-se-Bos served as a satellite for Tembelitsha, and another five-classroom school was being built in Bongani, the new, temporary township.

By 1983, Mam Tau's school was taking up to a hundred and eighty children. But it was still open only to the youngest children; the older ones had to walk to Witlokasie, a round trip of over twenty kilometres a day. Those were the children Owéna was most worried about. On wet winter days, many of them either stayed at home or left for school later in the day when it was warmer, missing out on most of their lessons as a result. The ones who did leave early enough often took their chances on the shortcut where children were assaulted and raped, the very reason Mam Tau had opened her school in the first place.

At the Thembalethu and Vulindlela committee meetings, the children's education came up time and time again.

Owéna listened as concerned parents complained about Tembelitsha and the lack of opportunities for their children. One of the big frustrations was that even the more ambitious children could only go so far. After years of offering only a primary education, Tembelitsha was eventually extended up to the junior secondary years of standards six and seven, or grade eight and nine. But that still left three years of schooling unaccounted for. Any black child who wanted to finish their school career had to go away to another town to do so. Some of them ended up in the Eastern Cape, where they stayed with relatives in townships, but most of them went to the nearer town of George. To get there, the Knysna children hitchhiked the sixty kilometres to George on Monday mornings and back on Fridays, missing most of their lessons on both those days. In George, those who didn't have family to stay with rented rooms from strangers in the townships and squatter camps.

But the majority of black parents in Knysna couldn't afford to send their children away. Instead, they made those children work so they could start bringing in money. As a result, most black children left school at the age of around fourteen and found jobs as manual labourers. In her first year of working in the squatter camps, Owéna had seen many a promising child end up with a drinking problem or a child of their own, often both.

In 1983, it was looking unlikely that Knysna would ever get a black secondary school. High schools needed almost twice as much land as primary schools; eight hectares compared to four. And when as many as twenty township houses could be built on just one hectare, a new school wasn't the government's biggest priority.

The government wasn't willing to put money towards Tembelitsha either, not when a school was being planned in the official township.

To make matters worse, it looked like Tembelitsha was about to lose five teachers.

From its earliest days, Tembelitsha struggled to attract and keep teachers. Besides the lack of facilities, the condition of the school buildings and the poor attendance record, the biggest deterrent was that the teachers had nowhere to live. It became even more difficult when the Bantu Administration ruled that no one was allowed to build any new houses in the squatter camps until the new township was completed. So strict were they about the new rule that when one of Tembelitsha's teachers tried to build a simple, one-roomed house, she was told to stop halfway through and break it down.

In 1983 there were five new, unmarried teachers at Tembelitsha with nowhere to live.

Owéna stepped in.

If one house could be built to accommodate all five of those teachers, so Owéna reasoned, surely the authorities could make a concession?

No, said the Bantu Administration. So Owéna went to the Department of Community Development. When they said no too, she went to the Knysna Municipality where she finally got her permission to build the teachers a house.

Having the permission was one thing, but there was no money for the house and no one in the black community was prepared to build it for free. Owéna got resourceful. For money, she appealed to the white people of Knysna. For materials, she went to local businesses. Everyone she approached gave generously, but free labour was still hard to find. People's pockets were more open than their schedules, it seemed.

Owéna went to the one man she knew she could talk into it.

Chapter 26

Theron

My father has always been a practical man, making and fixing things for as long as I can remember. My brothers grew up with handmade hobbyhorses, scooters, carts and periscopes from his workshop. I got wooden jewellery boxes, desks and bookshelves.

In that same workshop, my father lost a finger to a rotor blade when I was fifteen. I remember the night well: I was in my room when my mother called me to say she was taking my father to hospital. He had a bloody towel wrapped around his hand.

While cutting planks for wooden serving plates, he had managed to cut right down the middle of his little finger. At the hospital they said they could sew it back together, but that it would just be a stiff digit forevermore. My father said they'd better amputate it, because if he weren't able to use it, he would just end up cutting it off the next time anyway.

Like I said, my father has always been a practical man.

His handiwork can be seen all over my parents' house.

The wooden staircase. The cupboards and wardrobes. The kitchen table.

Also dotted around the house are various memorabilia from his days as a biology teacher. In the dining room, next to the old cashier's till under the cheque to Nobantu, there's a whale's eye in formaldehyde. Perched on a shelf in the kitchen next to jars of oats and rice, there's a horse embryo preserved in resin like an ancient fossil. And somewhere in his workshop downstairs he still has the jaw of a Great White shark that he caught many years ago, one of its teeth missing after a schoolboy stole it for a trophy necklace that would make him the envy of his surfer friends.

I used to take great pleasure in showing my father's macabre collection to my boyfriends, one of whom called us 'The Addams Family' as a result.

There were several more specimens in my father's classroom at Knysna High, where I was one of his students. Dog, cat, sheep and pig embryos lined the shelves around the room, suspended forever in their formaldehyde graves. There were living things, too: lizards and scorpions in vivariums, seahorses in aquariums.

My father believed in hands-on learning and we were always dissecting something or another in his class. We started with hibiscus flowers that we sliced into exact replicas of the cross-sections shown in our textbooks, to study under the microscope. By the time I got to my senior year we were dissecting birds; over-the-hill homing pigeons donated by a local farmer who had no use for them any more.

But when it came to my father's job at Knysna High, teaching was only half of it. He was also a handyman, a sports coach and a driver, ferrying hockey and rugby teams to away games. Every year for the school play he was in charge of the lighting, from working out the effects, to rigging it all up and operating the various spots on the night. He built the sets too; modular, wooden-framed canvas back-drops that could be transformed into living-room walls with slammable doors the one year, luscious midsummer forest scenes the next.

People still come to him when they need a creative solu-tion to a practical problem. Just last week, a friend asked him to devise some kind of hoisting mechanism for a bed for his mother-in-law, who had to sleep in a sitting position due to water on her lungs. My father came up with an ingenious pulley system, which was ready just a few days later.

If he was there for everyone else, my father was always there for us first. When my mother went back to work when I was little, it was my father who dropped me off and collected me from netball practice, tennis lessons and play rehearsals in the afternoons after school.

When I crashed my car as a student in Cape Town, my father was there within twenty-four hours to take it away and fix it. When that same car was stolen in Durban, my father made sure I had a new second-hand car within two days. He bought it and drove it to Durban, a thirteen-hour journey from Knysna that took him twenty hours back by coach.

He says in deeds what he doesn't say in words, never having been the most expressive of people. As a teacher he did get angry with some of the children, but when it comes to softer emotions, he tends to keep them in.

Growing up, I learned to read my father's body language, because it was often the only language he'd use. And so at prize-givings and graduations, I'd know he was proud of me by the little nod; the suppressed smile twitching at the corners of his mouth; the look in the other direction. These days I see that sideways look mainly at airports when we say goodbye.

In his retirement, my father spends most of his time and his talent making things to sell at a craft market near Knysna, where he and my mother have a stall called 'Theron's Wooden Goodies'. There are wheelie penguins on sticks for toddlers, for older children toy guns that shoot rubber bands, for their parents chopping boards and cheese plates made from indigenous wood from the Knysna Forest.

In everything he is meticulous: his planning, his measuring, his cutting, his sanding. We've all inherited it to some extent, my brothers and I. Our spouses are bemused at our aversion to an asymmetrical slice of bread, or an unbuttered corner of toast. Before I even went to school, I was able to draw a three-dimensional cube, taught by my father on a big blackboard on our kitchen wall.

It's still there, that blackboard, now covered in scribbles to illustrate whatever point my father was most recently trying to make to my mother.

Since I've been back here, I've offered to help my father sand some of the toys for the market, but he won't let me. Not even on Friday nights, when he goes through the usual last-minute panic that he won't have enough stock. It needs to be absolutely right, he says. The toy guns, for example, won't work if they're not sanded properly. All I'm allowed to do is 'load' the guns with rubber bands – enough of a low-risk task that he's willing to delegate it.

If my father is the craftsman at the stall, my mother is the saleswoman. Vivien jokes that my mother can sell snow to Eskimos. Maybe it's from all those years selling cookware.

My mother often uses her powers of persuasion on my father to rope him into her work. That's how he ended up helping her with her annual pancake stall at the Knysna Marathon, as he was doing again on the day of Queenie's funeral. This year, like every year, my father helped out the day before, putting up the tent with its Epilepsy South Africa banner and making sure the gas stoves were filled up and ready to go. That night I helped him with the other annual task: cutting a thousand sheets of greaseproof paper into many more thousands of smaller pieces that would become pancake wrappers the following day. In his workshop, I helped him balance the large reams of paper while he pushed them through a screeching band saw.

I asked my father how my mother talked him into doing all that work.

'She talks me into a lot of things,' he said.

Chapter 27

1983

Theron listened quietly as Owéna explained what needed to be done. Five basic rooms, she said. And they only had to last three years or so, until the township was built.

Theron never did say yes. He just went over to the black-board on the kitchen wall and started sketching dimensions for the teachers' house.

With all his commitments at school, Theron could only work on the house on Saturdays – and he couldn't build it alone. So he convinced his neighbour, an Englishman called Doug Starkey, to come along and help for free. Johnny came along too, paid by Theron for his time.

Theron also paid for the wood, his one condition being that he wanted it back after the three years were up.

When the black parents and teachers heard what Theron was doing, they insisted on helping to raise some money for the house. Child Welfare arranged a special evening of cheese, wine and music where the Tembelitsha school choir and the crèche children entertained a white audience who paid generously for the privilege.

But not everyone in the black community was as supportive of the house. From the day Theron first turned up at the building site with Doug and Johnny, a handful of young black men tried to intimidate them into going home. New ideas and ideals had been spreading around the squatter camps and young men, especially, were becoming disillusioned with their fate. In those men's eyes, the white men and their coloured labourer represented everything that was wrong with the country. And so they came and watched while Theron, Doug and Johnny worked, never offering to help, just standing and watching and talking among themselves.

Johnny could speak a little Xhosa, enough to understand what the men were saying. And it was clear that they didn't want them on their turf. Sometimes they spoke to Johnny directly, asking him what he and the white men were doing there and threatening them with 'trouble' if they didn't leave.

Whenever the young men seemed like they'd had just enough brandy to mean it, Johnny would tell Theron and Doug it was time to go. Theron, not wanting any trouble, would listen to Johnny and pack up for the day. When it happened more frequently, Johnny and Doug started working on the house during the week when it was quieter.

Then the wood that Theron was leaving at the building site started disappearing. Undeterred, Theron stored the planks at the nearby sawmill instead, bringing over just enough for the work he was doing that day, and making repeat trips to the sawmill if he'd underestimated.

Week after week, Theron, Doug and Johnny went back. And every time, there was someone telling them not to.

Even black teachers turned up with a few drinks in them sometimes; not the women who would eventually live in the house, but their male colleagues. Slurring their words, they demanded to know when the house would be finished, and why it was taking so long. But not one of them ever picked up a hammer to help.

Week after week for seven months, Theron, Doug and Johnny went back, until finally in November 1983, the house was finished. To celebrate, Child Welfare put on a tea party outside the house. All of Tembelitsha's staff turned up, as did several parents, who milled about admiring Theron and his team's work over tea and cake that Owéna had baked for the occasion.

From the other side of the road, a group of young black men stood watching without saying a word.

Chapter 28

Memories of apartheid

'Look, something had to change,' says my mother.

I'm asking my parents about the referendum of 1983 while we're having lunch at the kitchen table. I vaguely remember hearing about it then, but I was five years old and didn't even know what the word 'referendum' meant. Not that I ever cared for politics when I was older, either. It just wasn't something that came up in our house or, if it did, never in front of me.

I press my mother: what does she mean, 'something had to change'?

I'm expecting her to talk about the oppression of the black people, their suffering, their poor living conditions. So it comes as a surprise when her answer is from more of a white perspective.

'There were sporting boycotts and things,' she says. 'And it was so demoralising for the country that people like the Springboks couldn't compete internationally.'

My father adds: 'And then when the Springboks did tour, in New Zealand or Australia or somewhere, they dumped flour on them from a plane.'

Perhaps it shouldn't be so surprising that my parents use the rugby example first. Rugby isn't just our national sport, it's like a religion among white South Africans.

I've read about the controversial tour of New Zealand in 1981, where Springbok games were disrupted by protests and pitch invasions. The flour incident my father is talking about happened at the final game in Auckland.

As a child I wasn't aware of any of that, and I tell my parents so. My mother reminds me that I was very young, but I feel naive for only finding out about it now, when I'm thirty-one.

'Remember how we watched Zola Budd at the Olympics?' my mother asks.

I do. We all sat around the TV to cheer on the barefoot runner from Bloemfontein at the Los Angeles Olympics in 1984. If I realised at the time that Zola's vest wasn't the green and gold of our national colours, but the white, red and blue of Great Britain, I didn't question it. In my mind, as in all our minds, she was competing for South Africa. When Zola accidentally tripped American runner Mary Decker and got booed off the track, we hung our heads in national shame.

At least we had someone to cheer for at those Olympics; in most sports, South Africa wasn't represented at all. My parents made up for it by picking whoever they liked and supporting them instead. As a result, when I was little I just assumed Martina Navratilova and Ivan Lendl were South African.

'There was a cultural boycott too,' says my father. 'There were some films we couldn't get.'

'Yes, remember that?' my mother says, not to me but to my father, as if it's hard to believe now.

'And TV,' my father says. 'There was some British actors' organisation that boycotted us.'

I'm often reminded of the gaps in my TV knowledge now that I live in London. My husband was amazed to find out I hadn't grown up with shows like *Fawlty Towers* or *Blackadder*. We did get British children's TV like *Rupert the Bear* and *Postman Pat*, though.

'And artists couldn't come over to exhibit,' says my mother. 'Bands couldn't come and play.'

This time I can give her some examples. If there was one thing that affected me and my brothers, it was the cultural boycott that meant we couldn't see international bands and artists live.

When bands did eventually come over, it was a really big deal. I was fifteen when Orchestral Manoeuvres in the Dark played Plettenberg Bay Beach in 1993. It seemed all of Knysna was there, or at least all of white Knysna. OMD were supported by Mango Groove, a multi-racial and hugely popular local group that embodied the new South Africa.

My parents didn't feel the effects of the music boycott like we did, as they've always preferred classical music and opera. What did affect them, though, were the economic sanctions of the time.

'Companies pulled out of South Africa,' my mother says, clearing the table to make way for coffee. 'There were some products you couldn't buy.'

'Like French cars,' my father adds. 'And there was a petrol shortage, because countries wouldn't sell us oil any more. We could only get so much petrol at a time, I think it was five litres.'

'*Haai*, I remember,' says my mother, laughing. She obviously hasn't thought of those days for a long time.

'I think one of the petrol companies even pulled out of

175

South Africa,' says my father. 'A lot of companies did. So did Barclays.'

I remember Barclays Bank on the main street of Knysna 'becoming' First National Bank. At the time, I thought it had just changed its name. Years later, my first ad campaign as a young copywriter was to announce Barclays' return as an offshore bank. It was a tricky brief, as it turned out I wasn't the only South African who thought they'd never left.

So something had to change, I remind my parents, echoing my mother's earlier words.

She sits down next to my father and links her arm into his. 'Look,' she says, sounding more serious now. She takes a deep breath. 'When you worked up there, and you saw how they had *nothing*, then you could understand why those people got angry. Because when you sit in a house with no water, no electricity, and you're a whole family in just two rooms . . . There had to be a change.'

I remind her that the 1983 referendum wasn't going to change that, that the black people would remain disenfranchised whatever the result. I've been doing a lot of reading about the referendum in the last few weeks.

'Yes, but at least it was a step in the right direction,' says my mother.

Chapter 29

1983

The referendum was big news in Knysna. Everywhere Owéna looked, there was a poster or advertisement urging her to either 'Vote yes' or 'Vote no'.

As in the general elections, only white people would be allowed to vote. But the result of the referendum could change that for ever. A 'yes' vote would bring in a new constitutional framework giving coloured and Indian people limited representation in parliament – albeit still in separate chambers from their white peers. There, they would have a say in what the government called 'their own affairs', including education, social welfare, housing and recreation. In that so-called 'tricameral' parliament, coloured and Indian people would be allowed to vote for their own representatives. But, controversially, the black majority would still be neither represented nor consulted.

The National Party justified its decision to exclude black people by arguing they belonged in their homelands, where they had full voting rights among their own people. Its more liberal opposition, the Progressive Federal Party, or PFP, argued for the suffrage of the black majority, calling the proposed changes 'sham reform'.

Every week in the *Herald* there were full-page election ads sponsored by the National Party or the PFP. The National Party's campaign appealed to white South Africans' national pride with the rallying cry 'Vote yes. Put South Africa first.'

Theron read out the more divisive ads to Owéna, who responded with the occasional 'Oh, *please.*'

One 'Vote yes' advertisement said the new constitution would allow the country's 2.6 million coloureds and 821,000 Asians to 'participate in the process of democratic government', and that the constitution did not include the black nations because 'their constitutional development continued to progress along a different route'.

Despite disagreeing with the National Party's reasoning, Owéna and Theron both planned to vote 'yes'. Some change, they felt, was better than no change at all.

Many of their friends and neighbours were voting 'yes' for more personal reasons, as they told Owéna at school functions and fundraising events where every conversation inevitably led to the referendum.

It was the *swart gevaar*, they said – the 'black danger' that threatened the security and stability of the white people if the black majority were to come into power. And with that majority outnumbering the white population by around eight to one, who knew what would happen.

During those conversations, anyone who'd had friends and family in Rhodesia shared dramatic second-hand accounts of the horrors of black majority rule. The National Party stoked that fear in its campaigns. 'Think about your safety. Think about the safety of your children', said one of their ads. 'You only have to look north to see what happens when you have a system of "one man, one vote."'

Despite her own sister having fled Rhodesia when the changes happened, Owéna couldn't imagine South Africa going the same way. Not when she'd come to know the black people of Knysna. There were gentle, intelligent people up there in the squatter camps who would surely stop any trouble before it happened.

And yet the option of giving those people a voice was simply not on the table. Either coloured and Indian people got the vote, or no one did.

The debate raged on in the *Herald,* where the letters page, usually taken up with complaints about noisy speedboats on the lagoon and dogs fouling on Leisure Island, was almost entirely devoted to referendum views.

It's evolution, not revolution, said the 'yes' camp.

It's just for show, it's not real reform, said the 'no' camp.

If you vote 'no', you're effectively saying you don't want coloureds and Indians to be included in the democratic process, said the yeses.

Don't accept something that isn't good enough, said the nos.

Incensed Christians quoted Bible texts to support their argument, whichever side they were on.

On 2 November 1983, Owéna and Theron joined the queue of white voters outside the Knysna Town Hall.

Once inside, they were accosted by a PFP representative asking anyone voting 'no' to sign a petition rejecting apartheid as 'immoral, unjust and dangerous' and declaring their commitment to 'real, not sham, reform'. The declaration concluded by urging the prime minister to consult and negotiate with all leaders in South Africa so the country might have a constitution that encouraged and promoted 'security, justice and peace for all its citizens, irrespective of race or colour.'

Theron and Owéna still voted 'yes'. So did 66.3% of the electorate, giving the National Party the go-ahead it needed to start making the changes.

When Theron bought his next *Knysna-Plett Herald*, Prime Minister P.W. Botha was on the front page casting his vote at the Dutch Reformed Church in Wilderness, a small town between Knysna and his constituency of George.

Theron chuckled as he read the article to Owéna. Apparently, while television cameras and press photographers recorded the historic moment, 'cattle and sheep grazed peacefully around the hall while a small fluffy dog wandered around inside the hall.'

A week later, there was a letter from a reader responding to the P.W. Botha article.

It was from a Wilderness resident complimenting the paper on its 'fine reporting' of the prime minister's vote. There was just one little mistake, said the writer. 'The grass around our church hall was too short for cattle and sheep to graze on. The animals were on other residents' fields.'

Owéna laughed at the *Herald* reader's pedantic views.

But up on the hill, she knew there were thousands of people who had just been denied the right to have any kind of view at all.

Chapter 30

Johnny

I've always known Johnny to be quiet, keeping to himself while working in my parents' garden or eating his lunch in the shelter of the carport.

Johnny Oliphant has worked for my parents for thirty-five years now, coming down from Dam-se-Bos twice a week on Tuesdays and Fridays to do the gardening, clean the pool and help my father with whatever jobs need doing around the house.

Every time I see Johnny when I'm over from London, I greet him in the same way: with a hello and a hand raised in a stiff half-wave. He'll say hello back, with an even more awkward little wave. He'll ask how I'm doing, I'll say I'm doing well. I'll ask him the same question, he'll give me the same answer. 'That's good, that's good,' I'll say and go inside. That's pretty much the extent of our communication.

If I never became as attached to Johnny as to Queenie, it's because he was always outside the house. Even now, he still eats outside and uses the 'outside' toilet, a tiny room built onto the house but with a separate entrance. I never questioned why we even had that toilet until recently, when my father explained it was a legal requirement to have an outside toilet when they built the house. It was necessary so that builders or any other workers could access a toilet even when their employers were away and the house was locked up.

I now find it strange that Johnny still uses that toilet. When I ask my parents about it, they say he prefers it that way; that he gets sweaty and dirty working in the garden and so it's better if he goes outside. And anyway, my mother says, it's what he's used to. She doesn't think he'd feel comfortable using the toilets inside the house.

But Johnny doesn't just work outside any more. Since Queenie's first successor died a few years ago, he's been helping inside the house on Tuesdays, washing the dishes and the floors before heading out to the garden. Fridays he's in the garden all day and a new cleaner comes to do the rest of the house. My parents say they're pretty sure she uses the two toilets indoors, but they don't seem to mind.

One morning when my mother has gone to work and my father has gone to fetch Johnny, I go around the side of the house and try the door on Johnny's toilet. It's unlocked.

I haven't been in there for many years. The last time was when I was twelve, and a fan of the rock group Queen. Having exhausted my parents' collection of magazines, I took to Johnny's toilet in the hope of finding a picture of Freddie Mercury or Brian May in the old copies of *Huisgenoot* on the floor. Now there are no magazines, just a toilet and a sink. The walls could do with a coat of paint, but it's cleaner than I remember. I feel guilty for snooping and decide not to tell my parents that I've been in there.

When I tell Johnny I'd like to talk to him 'officially, for

the book', he suggests ten o'clock that morning so he's got enough time to do the dishes and mop the kitchen floor first.

I go down to the kitchen just as he's finishing up and sit down at the kitchen table with my notebook and a Dictaphone. Johnny doesn't sit down; instead he stands at the end of the table, leaning onto it as if he's just taking a brief break before getting back to his work.

'Sit, sit,' I say, indicating to one of the three empty chairs. His eyes widen and he sits down awkwardly. His back is dead straight, his hands are in his lap. He doesn't make eye contact. It occurs to me that he's probably never sat at our kitchen table. Come to think of it, there's a good chance he's never sat on any of the furniture in our house.

Johnny is dressed in his usual work outfit: a pair of blue overalls and a peak cap. The overalls look new. He's unshaven and his beard is greyer than I remember; so is the hair that sticks out from underneath his cap. His skin is dark, but I can make out a few freckles on his nose. I've never been close enough to him to notice them before.

Because Johnny is so dark and lives in the Dam-se-Bos squatter camp, I've always thought he was black. But recently my mother told me he's actually coloured. It was the opposite with Queenie: with her light skin I always thought she was coloured, but now I know she was 'technically' black.

Johnny couldn't be more different from Queenie. Whereas Queenie had an amazingly expressive way with words, Johnny struggles to find any words at all. He answers my questions mostly in single sentences, and I don't know whether it's down to a limited education or limited emotions.

Education certainly is an issue. Johnny tells me he only finished standard five, or grade seven. The school he went to in Harkerville, a small village between Knysna and Plett, didn't go higher than that. He started working when he was fourteen, first on a farm and then at a brick factory.

Johnny's younger siblings, on the other hand, all finished school in Hornlee, despite living in Dam-se-Bos – all except for one brother who died as a teenager. I never realised the Hornlee school was open to people living in the squatter camps, but Johnny says his brothers and sisters all got in easily, being coloured.

If Johnny's vocabulary is limited, his memory isn't. He remembers that he first started working for my parents in 1974, that my oldest brother was two years old at the time, and that my other brother and I weren't born yet.

Johnny specifically remembers how, as a toddler, my brother used to come and sit with him while he had his lunch outside. During those lunch breaks, he says, he'd feed my brother whatever soft food he had on his plate: pumpkin, sometimes mashed potato. Only the soft food, because my brother was so young.

I ask him whether my brother didn't bother him.

'It was all right,' he says. 'I know how children are.'

Johnny was the second oldest of ten children: seven boys and three girls. His mother, brothers and sisters moved to Knysna before he did.

Although the coloured township of Hornlee was just about finished at the time, Johnny's family was happy to squat in Dam-se-Bos. They had relatives there and had found a decent-sized piece of land on which to build a house.

Johnny initially came to Knysna from Harkerville just to help with the house. Five rooms it had, he says. A kitchen, sitting-room and three bedrooms that his mother and his nine brothers and sisters shared between them.

When Johnny eventually moved to Knysna, he built his own house in Dam-se-Bos, not far from his family.

Johnny still lives in that same house, which is due to be replaced with an RDP house under the government's Upgrading of Informal Settlements Programme.

I ask him how Dam-se-Bos has changed since he first came here in 1974.

'It's a bit messed up now,' he says. 'There are lots of people coming in. From other places. It wasn't as rough back then as it is now.'

I ask him where those people are coming from.

'From Transkei and places like that,' he says. 'Especially now that they're allowed to.'

I remind him that people were coming from the Transkei in 1974 too. What's the difference now?

'They come in so easily now,' he says. 'Then, they needed a pass. After a certain time, they had to go back. Now they get in easily. Now it's a bit messed up.'

I ask him what he means by 'messed up'.

People steal your money and hit you and rob you, he says. It's not safe to walk around at night.

Is it worse than before? I ask.

Much worse, he says. But now there are people you can go to if you've been robbed. 'People who'll find the robbers and give them a hiding', he says. 'But I don't know whether that helps either.'

I'm surprised to hear about the 'hidings'. Last year, in the UK, I saw a Louis Theroux documentary about black vigilantes in South Africa who catch and assault criminals in the townships, but that was in Johannesburg. I didn't think anything like that would happen in Knysna.

At least some things have moved on. There's electricity

in Dam-se-Bos now, says Johnny. 'You buy it,' he says. 'You buy ten rand, twenty rand, and when it's finished you buy another ten rand.'

I wonder how many nights he's been without electricity because he hasn't topped it up.

How about water? I ask him.

He's got a tap near him, he says. Next to the new community hall that's right near his house. He's been lucky, he says. Even when they just had tanks, those were right next to his house too. He's never had to walk far for water.

Johnny explains that it's possible to have water in the house now. You have to go to the municipality and tell them you want a tap on your plot. But then you have to pay.

I ask him what the people do for toilets when there's no running water in their houses.

'You have to dig your own toilet,' he says. 'Like a hole.'

I think of all those outhouses I've seen next to the shacks in Oupad and Dam-se-Bos, and imagine what they must be like inside.

I ask him about his outside toilet here at my parents' house. Is he happy to use it?

'Yes,' he says, 'I'm all right there.'

He says he's used to it.

We carry on like this for an hour, me asking a question, him answering in one, two sentences. Sometimes he says a bit more.

I ask him about his teenaged brother who died.

'He would have finished school that year,' Johnny says. 'He was on his way to becoming a traffic policeman. That was his plan.' He smiles at the memory of what his brother might have been. There's an older brother's pride in that smile, but there's a sadness too.

He remembers the school principal speaking at the funeral in Hornlee. 'The principal said very nice things,' he says.

I ask him how he felt when his brother died. His smile disappears.

'I felt bad,' he says.

He looks away.

Chapter 31

1984

Johnny ran all the way from Dam-se-Bos to Theron and Owéna's house to tell them the news.

His brother was dead.

It was early on a Tuesday morning and Theron hadn't left for school yet. He phoned to say he wouldn't be coming in that day.

The news of Johnny's brother didn't come as a surprise to Theron. Johnny had already been to see him two days before, the day after the fire.

It had happened on the Saturday night. Johnny had seen the flames from his house, but it was nothing unusual to see a shack fire in Dam-se-Bos. With no electricity, people relied on candles and oil lamps for light. When those fell over, it didn't take long for a wooden shack to burn to the ground.

Only when his girlfriend said it looked like his mother's house did Johnny start to panic.

He and the girlfriend ran over to where the flames were glowing in the night sky.

By the time they got there, the whole house was ablaze.

Neighbours were carrying over water in drums and buckets, but it made little difference. Someone said the Fire Department was on its way. Johnny saw his mother and ran over to her. She was lying on the ground away from the house and there were people around her. She was badly burned. Next to her was Johnny's brother, the third oldest of his mother's seven sons. He was in a much worse state.

Johnny's cousins, who lived nearby, had pulled his mother and brother out of the fire. But they were too late for the other two brothers who were still inside.

Johnny's girlfriend was hysterical. But Johnny didn't cry.

An ambulance came and took Johnny's mother and surviving brother away. Later that night, Johnny heard that his mother was in a stable condition in the Knysna hospital, but that his brother had had to be rushed through to Port Elizabeth, two hundred and fifty kilometres away. The boy was too badly burned, they said. He needed the kind of medical facilities that weren't available in Knysna.

When the news that his brother hadn't made it came on the Tuesday, Johnny got the message through an older brother, a detective in the Knysna police force. Johnny didn't know exactly when his brother had died, or even whether he'd made it to the hospital in Port Elizabeth. The message was just that the brother was dead. And his body had to be collected.

That was when Johnny ran to Theron.

Theron's parents were down from Cape Town and his father had a small Datsun bakkie that he could borrow for the day. It wasn't ideal, but it had to do. Theron took Johnny to the Knysna police station, where they got an official declaration giving them permission to collect the body from the morgue in Port Elizabeth. Their next stop was the local undertaker in Knysna where Theron bought a simple coffin, the kind used for paupers' burials. Finally they went to a service station, where they put as much petrol in the bakkie as they were allowed under the restrictions. It was enough to get them where they were going.

With the declaration in the glove-box of the bakkie and the coffin on the back, Johnny and Theron set off for Port Elizabeth. A harbour city in the Eastern Cape with a big car manufacturing industry, Port Elizabeth, or 'PE' as the locals called it, was a three-hour drive away from Knysna. As the Eastern Cape didn't have the coloured labour preference of its Western neighbour, it had a considerably bigger black population.

And that black population was getting restless.

Theron had seen the reports on the news. Protests had broken out in the Transvaal province earlier that month and were spreading to the Eastern Cape. In the aftermath of the referendum of the year before, people were unhappy about the introduction of new black local governments, which were seen as poor substitutes for black representation in the new tricameral parliament. And they were starting to demonstrate their anger in increasingly violent ways.

The police station in Port Elizabeth where Johnny's brother's body was being kept was on the edge of a black township. A high fence topped with spiky spirals of barbed wire kept the people from the police and the police from the people.

Theron noticed that the young policemen, most of them black, looked tense. Walking back and forth along the fence, they ran the handles of their long, black leather whips called *sjamboks* along the wire in a threatening, metallic rattle.

Every so often, one of them whipped the fence with his *sjambok*.

The policemen reminded Theron of soldiers in the Angola border war. Theron hadn't fought in the war himself; his bad eyesight had prevented him from going. But he'd once seen a documentary of how those soldiers were shown photographs of chopped-up animals and human bodies to desensitise them.

That was how those policemen looked to him: desensitised and ready to kill.

Theron didn't want to stick around longer than he had to. But he and Johnny wouldn't be going home anytime soon.

The declaration from the Knysna police wasn't enough to get them the body. The Port Elizabeth police said they could hand it over, no problem – but for Theron to take it all the way back to Knysna, he needed a permit to transport a corpse.

For the rest of the day, he and Johnny were sent from one government department office to the next until finally they got the piece of paper they needed.

By the time they got back to the police station, the morgue was closed.

Theron was furious. With a red face usually brought on only by the most disobedient children at school, he convinced the policeman at the front desk to call the morgue supervisor at home.

An hour later, the supervisor turned up, a big black man with beer on his breath. Theron, sensing it was the only way to get the body and get out of there, apologised with feigned humility for making him come all the way there.

It worked. After some macho grumbling, the supervisor

let Theron and Johnny into the morgue where he left them to get the body into the coffin themselves.

When they loaded the coffin onto the bakkie, it was getting dark. The policemen were still there at the fence, pacing with their *sjamboks*.

A week later, Johnny's brother was buried along with the other two who'd never made it out of the burning house. Johnny was there with his remaining brothers and sisters, but his mother was still in hospital and never got to bury her sons.

Johnny cried then. But just a little bit.

Chapter 32

1986

Shack fires became increasingly common and their effects more severe as the squatter camps grew. With more shacks packed onto small areas of land, a fire that started in one could quickly spread to the next one along, and the one next to that. Every time it happened, Owéna was up there with donations of blankets, clothes, shoes and food to help the newly homeless families get by.

Undeterred, the black workers kept coming to Knysna in the hope of making a living. And when Influx Control was abolished in January 1986, their wives and children started coming with them.

Owéna, or *Nobantu* as she had been christened by the people, noticed the increase in black families in Knysna. In particular, she noticed the rise in the number of older, unskilled black women. She met several of those women during her visits to the squatter camps, and it worried her that most of them stayed at home doing nothing but look after their grandchildren, collect firewood and cook for their families. In the paternalistic Xhosa culture where the man was king, that was all that was expected of their women.

Owéna couldn't stand seeing bright minds paralysed by a lack of stimulation. Some of the women became crèche mamas and so at least gained some skills. But for many more, their shacks and their immediate surroundings were their whole world; the babies on their backs their only company.

Owéna went to Miss Broster with an idea. Child Welfare could sponsor an activity group to teach the women basic sewing and craft skills, so they could make things to sell and supplement their pitiful pensions. All she needed were some volunteers to run the group.

As soon as Miss Broster suggested Lois Bubb, Owéna knew she'd be perfect.

Owéna had met Lois at Loeriehof, a white care home for the elderly where Owéna sometimes dropped in to give books to people who were too frail to get to the library.

Lois's mother was one of those people, and it was at her bedside that Owéna and Lois first got talking. She had a feistiness that immediately appealed to Owéna. Lois was fifty-seven years old and suffered from multiple sclerosis. She had recently been confined to a wheelchair, but she didn't let her disability get her down.

When Owéna invited Lois to run the black women's group, Lois not only accepted, she also volunteered two more friends to help out, as well as suggesting a venue: the Kupugani food depot, where she had been doing voluntary work for the previous two years. All that was left for Owéna to do was spread the word.

★

At the agreed time on the agreed day, Owéna, Lois and the other two volunteers sat eagerly watching the clock in the Kupugani food depot. They had chairs and stools, which they'd packed out in a neat circle. They had needles, thread and scraps of fabric. They had a bucket of vitamin-enriched orange squash and plenty of plastic cups.

They waited.

Ten minutes, twenty minutes, thirty minutes after the agreed time, the women came. One by one, sometimes two by two, they filed in to the Kupugani food depot and took their places on the chairs and stools. Most of the crèche mamas were there; some had sent their apologies. Others brought their neighbours. There was no need to find extra seats, but Owéna was pleased to see there weren't many empty seats either.

She was even more pleased to hear the sound that filled the room: the sound of women talking, laughing and sharing news. Owéna welcomed them, a translator repeating after her for those women who only spoke Xhosa.

First things first, said Owéna. They needed a name for the group. The women made suggestions, debated and deliberated. It wasn't often they were asked for their opinions.

'Masakhane,' they finally agreed. "'To help each other.'"

In the weeks that followed, Owéna left Lois to run the Masakhane group, just checking in now and then to see if they needed anything. Whenever she did, she was struck again by the laughter in the room.

She also noticed that the chairs were having to be more tightly packed in, and before long she had to move the group to Flenterlokasie, where the church leaders offered up the Red Church as a new venue.

There, the Masakhane women continued to sew and stitch and knit. Sections of patchwork hand-stitched over weeks came together to make entire bedspreads. Fabric and stuffing became dolls for grandchildren.

Some of the more ingenious ideas for crafts came from Lois who, as a child of the Great Depression, had a habit of keeping and recycling whatever she could. Before long the Masakhane women were plaiting together old stockings and laddered pantyhose into coiled bathmats, and crocheting plastic supermarket bags into handbags and sun hats. Some items they kept for themselves, others they sold.

Several of the Masakhane women started specialising in a specific skill, like Mama Zina, who made intricate patchworks using only the smallest pieces of fabric for the biggest variation in colour. Lois and the volunteers always sat among the black women, sewing their own things to use as examples. They weren't teachers, they weren't separate, they were women just like them.

As well as creative skills, Lois and Owéna taught the Masakhane women life skills, such as how to work out household budgets to make their money go further.

Then along came Lois with an idea that combined both the creative and life skills: the 'Wonder Box'. She showed Owéna one that she'd bought at a Cape Town welfare organisation called Compassion.

Owéna loved it.

By all appearances, the Wonder Box was just a large cardboard box with two bean bags in it. But in practice, it was actually a clever, fuel-free slow cooker. Once brought to the boil on a stove, a pot of food could simmer away for hours between the bean bags.

It worked particularly well for staple starches like maize,

porridge, dried beans and rice, making it ideal for African people. And it was cheap and easy to make, which made it ideal for the Masakhane women.

What convinced Owéna most was that it could help prevent shack fires, as the women would no longer need to keep their wood-fired stoves on all night.

At the next Masakhane group, Lois introduced the Wonder Box.

Owéna watched the women's faces as they gathered around Lois and her cardboard box. Some of them looked sceptical, but all of them were curious.

Lois explained each step of the process in the simplest language. Now she's heating rice and water in a pot on a gas stove. Now she's putting the warm pot in the box, on top of the bean bag. The second bean bag goes on top of the pot. Now she's putting the lid back on the box.

The women looked disappointed when Lois said that was it for the time being, that they could carry on with what they were doing.

After an hour, Lois called them back to the box and asked Mama Zina to lift the lid off the pot.

As soon as Mama Zina's fingers touched the metal, she jumped back. *Shu-Shu!* she said. Hot–hot!

Inside the pot, the rice was perfectly cooked. The women laughed and clapped their hands together.

It is a magic box, said Mama Zina. The rest of the women agreed. They would make the magic box for their people.

It didn't take Owéna long to find the necessary materials, most of them for free. She convinced a packaging company in Port Elizabeth to make the boxes, complete with the word 'Wonder Box' printed on the sides. She got her sister to donate old shirting from the clothing company she worked for in Cape Town. And from Knysna's furniture and appliance shops, she got the redundant polystyrene from boxes once their contents had been unpacked for display.

The Masakhane women got productive. Boxes were put together with assembly-line efficiency. Shirting was cut and sewn into bean bags. Polystyrene was grated into snowy flakes for the stuffing.

In the squatter camps, their neighbours marvelled at the finished product. Women, especially, loved the idea of being able to put on a pot of porridge in the evening and have it ready and hot for their husband's breakfast in the morning. No more getting up at sunrise or spending the night worrying about their shack catching fire.

But somehow the Wonder Box never caught on.

Some people said it was just too neat, with its fancy, printed box and its pristine cushions.

They didn't want to spoil it by using it.

Chapter 33

Lois Bubb

'Eight women made that,' says Lois.

She points at her bedspread, a technicoloured patchwork of stripes and flowers and polka dots and African prints in blues, yellows, pinks and greens. No two scraps of fabric are the same size or shape, and stitches of varying precision are clearly visible.

The bed is the metal kind on wheels that you get in hospitals. It's right here in the front room where we've been having our tea. Lois doesn't use the rest of the house much any more. She presses a button and her electric wheelchair starts beeping like a reversing truck. She's trying to get back to the table where we've been sitting, and it takes a five-point turn just to turn around.

I've known Lois since I was little, when my mother often took me along to the Masakhane group in the afternoons after school. Despite the wheelchair, I remember her manoeuvring around the uneven surfaces of the squatter camps with ease.

Having made her way back to the table, Lois takes a sip

of the tea her black carer has brought us. Her full lips pucker in her pale, wrinkled face.

'You know, a human being is a human being,' she says. She talks slowly, with long pauses.

'I will always remember something I saw in Cape Town about fifty years ago,' she says. 'A blind man was walking with a white stick. And as he started crossing the road, a coloured woman, a sort of washerwoman type, she helped him. And he said, "Thank you, my child," and he took her hand and he kissed it. And she said, *"Maar ek is bruin, meneer."* But I am brown, sir. And I remember him saying, "My girl, colour does not come off."'

She smiles, her eyes narrowing into crinkled slits.

'Colour does not come off.'

Born in 1929 to devout Nationalist parents, Lois has eighty years of stories to tell. I ask her how the daughter of two Nationalists ended up like her, a fighter for human rights who once ended up in prison for protesting as a student.

'It comes back to that painting,' she says, pointing to a framed picture on the wall that depicts thatched African mud huts in pretty pastel colours.

'I call it *The Rape of My Africa.*'

When she was a little girl in Pretoria in the 1930s, says Lois, the men who worked in the streets doing the 'pick and shovel' work were not black, they were white. So were most of the labourers on her grandfather's farm, where she spent her Christmases as a child. There were some black labourers on the farm, she says, but they worked mainly with the livestock. They lived in mud huts like those in the painting.

'Because remember,' she says, 'the blacks were a rural people.'

A little purse-lipped smile crinkles her face.

'And there was no hunger,' she says. 'Every hut had its ground with it. They had chickens, there was the odd pig, there was milk from cows. They would stamp dried corn into maize meal. They had dried beans, peas . . . Everybody ate well, out of the ground.

'But then you got somebody who came with a little brick house with a corrugated iron roof. And it had windows and it had doors. You can see them in the painting there.'

I look at the painting again. There they are, three angular, flat-roofed houses in the background that I hadn't noticed before.

'And what happened?' says Lois. 'The women said, "We want houses like that." And what did the men do? They went to go and work in the mines. Because these brick houses, they had to pay for them. Before, they didn't have to pay for the mud to build their huts. They didn't have to pay for the sticks for the framework. They didn't have to pay for the grass for the thatching, or for the manure to add to the clay for the floor of the hut. There was very little that they had to have money for, until they saw these brick houses.'

A pause, a sip of tea.

'That's why I call that painting *The Rape of My Africa*,' she says. 'It's that almost capitalistic element that came in, when money became important.'

I'm not sure how this relates to my question about how she ended up being so left wing when her parents were so right. I try to bring her back from the 1930s but she prefers to stay right there.

'I had a friend on my grandfather's farm, a black boy called Kondeki. He was about my age and lived in one of those huts,' she says, pointing at the painting again. 'Kondeki understood about snakes and scorpions and things like that and we were pals.'

She takes a bite of a rusk from the packet I brought along, her hand moving in slow motion. When she carries on talking, the dry biscuit muffles her words.

'One day we were playing, me and Kondeki, and my grandfather was sitting on these steps at the farmhouse. He had a permanent stiff leg from being shot in the knee in one of the so-called *kaffir* wars.'

I wince at the K-word. According to my South African English dictionary, it's now an actionable offense to use it. Derived from the Arabic word for 'unbeliever', it was a generic term for black people that the European settlers used when they first came into contact with them. During apartheid, the word became highly derogatory; as offensive as the word 'nigger' in the United States, if not more.

The wars she's referring to were the conflicts between the Xhosa people and white settlers in the nineteenth century.

I wonder if Lois's historical context and the added 'so-called' makes the K-word OK.

Lois doesn't seem to notice my discomfort. Her eyes are looking at something I can't see. Something a long time ago.

'So my grandfather called me and Kondeki over,' she says. 'And he talked to us about respect. About respect for yourself, about the meaning of respect. And he said to me, "When you grow up, you will be Kondeki's boss. And Kondeki will be your servant. But if you don't respect Kondeki and Kondeki does not respect you, you will have a bad servant. And the foundation of that respect comes from yourselves. You have to live with yourselves, you have to respect yourselves in order to respect somebody else."'

Lois blinks and sees me again.

'And that is a lesson I have absorbed more and more the older I get.'

Kondeki ended up working on the railways, she says. Not in any important position, just as a manual worker. There he died, on the railways.

'I think it was also that lady over there,' says Lois, remembering my original question about the influences that made her so radical.

She's pointing at an old photographic portrait that looks like it was taken not long after the camera was invented. 'That's my mother's mother, who taught me to do unto others as you would have them do unto you. That, plus my grandfather's – my father's father's – concept of respect.'

Since then Lois has spent her life challenging the status quo, even at a time when just questioning it could get you in trouble.

She's convinced that her political views got her kicked out of Stellenbosch University. Having passed her first year in medicine with good results, she missed the minimum year mark for her second year by one percentage point, meaning she wasn't allowed to write her exams.

'When I queried my mark,' she says, 'I ended up before a panel who said to me, "Miss, if we don't stop you now, you will only cause problems for us."'

Many years later Lois found herself in Swellendam, a small town between Knysna and Cape Town where she worked at the local museum and volunteered at the Red Cross. When the chairman of the Red Cross died, Lois was appointed in her place.

Lois insisted that all of the Red Cross committee members, including the coloured sub-committee, put in an appearance at the late chairman's funeral. But when she turned up at the Dutch Reformed Church with two of her coloured colleagues, she was told that 'brown people can go and sit in the gallery'.

Lois insisted they come inside with her.

'There was a hell of a to-do about it,' says Lois. 'And I said OK, fine, then I'll go to the newspapers. It's your choice.'

After much flustering, the Dutch Reformed Church's welcoming committee let them in.

'So I walked in with two coloured ladies and we sat down,' says Lois, 'a mixture of brown and white in the Dutch Reformed Church.'

She beams at the memory of her victory.

Swellendam was a conservative town, says Lois. She still has a fork that someone threw away, 'just because a brown person had used it'.

Come to think of it, says Lois, her own mother was almost the kind of person who'd throw away a fork because a brown person had used it.

I'm not surprised that Lois has kept the fork after all these years. She's an astonishing hoarder. On my last trip to Knysna from London, I spent a whole afternoon looking through the top of a dusty wardrobe in her spare room, rifling through boxes full of notebooks and papers and leaflets and magazines. I left with two boxes of notebooks stuffed full of handwritten meeting minutes and annual reports from Child Welfare dating back to 1939, and the same for the Ladies Benevolent Society. Lois had salvaged them to use, someday, to write Child Welfare's history.

It was a treasure trove at a time when I found little other documentary evidence of Knysna's past.

Lois used to be very involved with Child Welfare, which

is why I'm here today. She was even given her own Xhosa name in a ceremony similar to my mother's.

Unable to remember what her Xhosa name – Nolunthu – means, Lois calls her carer over.

The carer struggles to explain the meaning in English. 'When you love someone,' she says. '*U*lunthu . . . and *No*lunthu . . . it's a very lovely name,' she says, giving up on the literal translation.

'Well, that's my Bantu name,' says Lois.

'Whoo!' says the carer. It seems this is news to her. 'That's very nice. That name means a lot.'

Lois looks pleased.

I feel bad changing the topic, but the fork story has reminded me of something I wanted to ask. Does she have any photos or newspaper clippings from the time she spent volunteering in the townships?

She thinks for a long time. She might have some, she says.

She makes another stop-start turn to go to the spare room, calling the carer to come and help.

From her wheelchair, Lois directs me and the carer as we lower two heavy boxes from the top of the wardrobe. 'No, not that one. The one next to it.' She points with a crooked finger. 'Yes, that one.'

I flick through yellowed notebooks and papers while the carer is asked to look through the linen inside the wardrobe. My search is unsuccessful; one of the boxes seems entirely filled with detailed drawings and plans for horse-drawn carts and wagons, presumably from Lois's museum days. The other offers up a random selection of dressmaking patterns and 1970s women's magazines, interspersed with folders full of letters and notes that I stop reading when I realise they're from doctors.

The carer is more successful on her mission.

'Is this what you're looking for?' she asks Lois, holding up a cushion cover with the same colourful patchwork as the bedspread in the front room, only made from much smaller scraps of fabric. 'That's the one,' says Lois. She takes the cover and strokes it flat on her lap. 'Mama Zina made this one.'

Beep, beep, beep, beep. On her way out the door, Lois says the light is better in the front room, in case I want to photograph the cushion cover. I duly take the pictures, first on the table where Lois lays it out for me, then on Lois's lap so I can take some shots of her, this old white woman holding a patchwork cushion cover made for her by an old black woman a long time ago.

When it's time to leave, I ask Lois whether she wants me to put the cushion cover back in the wardrobe.

'No,' she says. 'Just put it there on the rocking chair for now. I'll find a cushion for it.'

I put the cushion cover on the chair next to the bed with its matching bedspread, reuniting Mama Zina with the eight women of Masakhane.

Chapter 34

1986

The unrest seemed to start almost overnight.

One day Owéna was driving into the squatter camps to take sewing supplies to the Masakhane women; the next she was stopped by police barricading the road. The police let her through, as she was in the Child Welfare bakkie and they'd been given orders to let the Welfare in. The only other vehicles allowed in were the municipality's water tanker to top up the supplies in the squatter camps, and ambulances to get the sick and the injured out.

Owéna wasn't prepared for the scenes on the other side of those barricades. Cars were in flames on the side of the road and she had to swerve to avoid burning trees blocking her way. A crowd of people came towards the bakkie, waving sticks and bricks in the air. When they recognised her, they let her through with fisted salutes and calls of '*Amandla!*' – 'Power!'

Owéna returned the salute, unaware of its political significance as a unifying gesture of the uprising that was spreading across the country.

★

In Knysna, it was the teenagers returning from school and university in the Eastern Cape who were igniting the fire in their people's minds. They came back with stories of a man called Mandela in a prison called Robben Island. Of children being killed by police, shot dead. They spoke of apartheid. Oppression. The struggle.

They didn't have to take it, said the children to their friends and their fathers. There was an uprising starting in South Africa, and it was time for the people of Knysna to join it.

Though the police were suddenly more visible in the squatter camps, in truth the unrest had been a long time coming.

Owéna had been hearing about sporadic outbreaks of violence, often against the municipality's workers. Both the black community and the white people in town were talking about young men throwing stones at firemen trying to fight shack fires. Even hearses were being attacked during funeral processions through the squatter camps. Eventually the firemen and municipal workers refused to go into the squatter camps after dark.

Owéna kept going in, even after the riots started. More than ever, she had to make sure the people were all right. It was her job. But she was also energised by the experience, the thrill of it appealing to a sense of adventure she'd never realised she had.

Occasionally she got a phone call from a crèche mama warning her that 'it's not a good day', which usually meant that a clash between the police and the people had broken out, making it too dangerous to go up there. On those days, Owéna stayed in her office.

She never actually worried for her own safety. But Theron

did. Owéna tried to reassure him that it was fine, that the people wouldn't hurt her. They knew her, and they knew the Child Welfare bakkie. They were just children, the same ones she'd been working with all those years.

But those weren't the people Theron was worried about. It was the instigators, people who were coming in to Knysna and putting ideas in the local kids' heads. Those people didn't know Owéna.

Theron couldn't stop Owéna going up there. But every time she did, he watched the clocks and listened for the phone, bracing himself for a call from the police or the hospital with bad news.

Theron saw the Casspirs before Owéna did, one morning on his way to school. A line of the yellow armoured vehicles was crawling up the hill past Knysna High, and Theron knew they had to be on their way to Witlokasie.

He called Owéna as soon as he got to school.

'*Now* there's trouble,' he said.

Chapter 35

Amy Matungana

I've been asking around for names of people who were actively involved in the unrest of 1986; people who can tell me what it was like in the squatter camps at the time.

One name keeps coming up: Amy Matungana.

Vivien was the first to suggest her. 'Now *she* can tell you a few stories,' she said.

These days Amy is the ward councillor for part of Khayalethu, which means she represents the community on the town council. She's also the councillor for my parents' neighbourhood, Upper Old Place, which falls into her ward. This surprises me, as I assumed my parents' councillor would be someone more local to Old Place and so, I supposed, more white.

Amy's house is in Khayalethu, around the corner from Queenie's. When I drive up there, it's the first time since Queenie's funeral that I'm going to the township by myself.

It's a jovial woman who answers the door and sits me down on a sofa in her living room. Amy is a real storyteller full of anecdotes, which she tells me through smiles and laughter. Sometimes when she laughs, it's accompanied by a deep cough and she apologises, explaining that she hasn't been well.

We talk about Queenie who, it turns out, had more in common with Amy than just being her neighbour. Like Queenie, Amy was raised as coloured when she was actually black. And like Queenie, she married a black man from the Transkei. But unlike Queenie, Amy wanted to be black all her life.

'Growing up, I always had a longing to mix with the black people, the Xhosa people,' she says. 'I never found the coloured people interesting enough . . . When we went to social events, I wanted to go where there were black people.'

I ask her what made the black culture so appealing.

'Your blood goes back to where you've come from,' she says.

Amy didn't always know she was Xhosa. Born Jackson and raised to speak Afrikaans, she went to coloured schools where her dark skin provoked taunts of '*swartmens*' – black person – and '*kaffir*'.

'I cried,' she says. 'Because I didn't grow up as one, I didn't believe I was one, and I didn't have any knowledge of my history. It made me very sad when someone said, "You're not a coloured, you're something else."'

Only when she started looking into her family history did she realise that her ancestors weren't Jackson but Njemlo, a surname they changed first to the more Afrikaans-sounding Jansen before settling on Jackson.

Now that she's older, Amy realises why her family did what they did; that they weren't the only people to change their identities in an attempt to avoid the consequences of being black in South Africa.

'But I'm proud to be black now,' she says. 'Very proud.'

It wasn't an easy transition, though. Shortly after she married her husband, Alvin Matungana, she got her first real taste of what it was like to be black.

It was 1984 and Amy went to the Knysna magistrate's office to apply for her learner's driving licence. The woman behind the counter looked her up and down and said, 'What do you want to do with a licence?'

Amy remembers the incident vividly. 'This white lady said to me, "The petrol is so expensive and the cars are so expensive, tell me what do you want to do with a driving licence?" And I said to her, "Exactly what you do with your one."'

At the time Amy still had an identity card, which was only issued to coloured people, not black. But the card said Jackson, not Matungana. That was enough for the clerk. 'She said to me you're married now, you're Matungana, you can't have an ID, you must go and get a passbook,' says Amy. 'And she told me she'd make sure I didn't get a driving licence unless I changed my surname to Matungana.'

When it came to collecting her licence, Amy, who worked as a cleaner, asked her white employer to go along. 'I said to her you'd better come with me,' says Amy, 'because otherwise I might not come back from that magistrate's office today because I'm not going to keep my mouth shut and they're going to lock me up.'

Amy remembers what happened when they got to the front of the queue. 'I handed over my things and I stood there, and I don't know if it was because there was a white person with me, but the lady didn't say anything.'

Her husband, Alvin, was having an even harder time. A labourer from the Eastern Cape with no permit to work in Knysna, Alvin couldn't get a job. Amy's employer's husband tried going to the Bantu Administration saying he wanted Alvin to work for him as a gardener, but the application was turned down on the grounds that there were other people with permits who could do the job.

So Alvin stayed at home, hiding whenever the Bantu Administration van came past, while Amy carried on doing domestic work and being the breadwinner in the family.

They had every reason to be frustrated. But they couldn't say anything. 'In those days our mouths were gagged,' says Amy. 'We couldn't say much and we couldn't do what we wanted. So everything we did back then was a bit under-ground.'

She tells me how the black people started meeting in secret, at night. At those meetings, they shared what they knew about what was going on in the rest of the country, and what they might be able to do to demonstrate their frustration to the white people. At the end of each meeting, they sang songs. 'You know,' she says, but I don't. 'Songs that egg you on a bit, that give you a bit of spirit. That said things like "this place belongs to our parents" or "what did we do to deserve this?" Sometimes they made up a song. They were good at that.'

She tells me there were rules for those meetings. They were always at someone's house, but never in the same place two nights in a row. People were nominated to host the meetings. And once you were nominated, you couldn't refuse.

'You didn't have a choice,' she says. 'The community where you lived said you had to do this and that and you just had to do it. And then the young people say to you,

"Tonight we're coming together at your house," and you can say what you want, but they're going to come with their chanting and their singing, and then you must open your house for a meeting.'

I ask her if the police ever turned up to break up those meetings.

'No, actually. The people always scattered before the police could get them. That's why they changed venues like that, from one house to the next.'

I'm curious to know where the politics came from, as Knysna always seemed so peaceful.

'Most of the black people in Knysna back then were from the Eastern Cape and the Transkei,' she says. 'And that's where the gatherings happened and the talking happened about having to do something about the situation.

'As you say, Knysna was peaceful. But it had also gained quite a few black people. And Knysna's children, our children, were now mixing with guys at the high schools and universities and things were discussed there.'

So what sparked the unrest here?

'I think it's as it is now,' says Amy. 'It starts in one place and it ends up all over the country. Like now, they've started complaining about service delivery, so in all the towns you can see it's burning and it's going on. And the one town ignites the next. I think that's what happened.'

She looks at her watch and says she needs to go pick up someone from the hospital.

'You can come along if you want,' she says.

The Knysna hospital is a short drive from Khayalethu, back towards town. We pick up a passenger on the way, the sister of the man we're collecting.

At the hospital, the two of them go in, leaving me in the car. After a while Amy reappears alone, saying the patient is on his way.

While we wait, I ask her how she feels about the situation in Knysna now.

She thinks for a long while, then says: 'I think the atmosphere is much better than before. I think the municipality has done a lot for Knysna's people. And I think we're still busy giving people the best we can give. If I'm speaking on behalf of the council, the council is planning to do the best in its ability to keep the people of Knysna happy.'

'Do the people appreciate it?' I ask.

Again, there's a pause before she answers.

'I wouldn't say many of our black people appreciate what's already been done,' she says. 'But I think their eyes are starting to open. People are only now starting to understand how it works: we can't build houses if we don't get money from the provincial government. Provincial gives the money, the housing board approves . . . In the past, people didn't know those things. And all the blame came to the municipality of Knysna.'

The patient and his sister emerge from the hospital. He looks like it hurts to walk and gets in the back of the car with his sister. I try to tell him he should sit in front, but Amy says it's fine. The man doesn't say anything.

When we get to the traffic light where the hospital approach joins the main road, there's a bang on the window. It's a man on crutches wanting a lift back to the township. He knows Amy and however much she objects – 'I've *already* got a sick man in the back' – he won't take no for an answer. When the traffic light stays red and the man keeps pleading, Amy gives in.

The man joins the other two passengers in the back. It's a squeeze and I feel even worse now about sitting in the front. And still the light doesn't turn green.

Our new passenger is more talkative than the other two.

'It's terrible what's happened to *Ma* Koti, isn't it?' he says. My ears prick up.

He must be talking about Elizabeth Koti, another black ward councillor who I spoke to on my last trip. I've been hoping to have a follow-up interview with her this time, as she, like Amy, was involved behind the scenes of the unrest. But the timing hasn't been ideal. Her husband died shortly before I arrived in Knysna, and my mother, knowing that Xhosa widows are expected to observe a strict and lengthy mourning period, has recommended I leave it a while before I call.

'Yes,' says Amy, but she doesn't elaborate.

The passenger does. 'I hear she had the police guarding her house all of Sunday night.'

I realise they're not talking about Elizabeth's husband dying.

Amy doesn't go into detail, but the man in the back chips in with some supplementary comments. From what I can tell, it all comes back to the 'service delivery' that Amy mentioned earlier. Apparently the community in Elizabeth's ward has been unhappy about how long it's taking to get houses and electricity, and it all came to a head on Sunday when a mob of people marched to Elizabeth's house and threatened to burn it down.

Amy doesn't seem to want to talk about it, although it might just be the traffic light making her impatient. It's been red now for a long time.

I point out what I've suspected all along: that the light

won't change until she edges forward to set off a trigger designed to give ambulances instant access from the hospital grounds to the main road.

Amy follows my advice and the light turns green.

'You learn something every day,' she says.

I don't ask any more questions until after we've dropped off the three passengers. With the back seat empty and Amy's house just around the corner, I press her on the recent events one last time.

'Aren't you worried that the guys in Khayalethu will get unhappy too and start threatening you?' I ask, referring to the people in her ward.

Amy keeps her eyes on the road, looking unfazed.

'If they want to be unhappy then they must be unhappy,' she says. 'I did what I could. I've always tried to make them happy and keep them happy.'

But are they empty threats, or will the people really do something?

'They'll really do something,' she says.

I press a bit more. Will they really go ahead and burn things, even houses?

'Yes,' she says. 'Our guys have that spirit. That wind. They'll really do something.'

Chapter 36

Trouble

My father has come upstairs to find me in my room where I'm piecing together the growing timeline on the wall. I'm up to February 1986.

'There's been trouble up there,' he says.

I know immediately that he's talking about the townships.

It's Friday morning and my father has just got back from picking up Johnny. That's where the trouble was, in Dam-se-Bos, at Elizabeth Koti's house. It's not far from Johnny's.

My father says they've been burning things up there; that there are still things burning.

'Do you want to go and have a look? I'll take you.'

I accept his offer to drive me there. This is one time I don't want to go to the townships alone.

We've barely turned off the N2 towards Dam-se-Bos when we see the first evidence of last night's events: long, black tracks on the road like skid marks after a car accident. My father says it's where they rolled burning tyres down the hill.

Trouble

'The burning rubber makes a hell of a lot of smoke,' says my father. 'That's why they burn tyres; it looks really dramatic.'

Crawling up the road in the hard shoulder is a digger carrying a smouldering load of what looks like branches of a large tree and rubbish. As we drive past, I notice a little flame still licking away at the leaves.

At the turn-off to Johnny's house there's a *shebeen*, as the bars in the townships are called. The dirt path outside it is littered with broken bottles – many more than usual. Nearby there's a road sign that's been ripped out of the ground. Its wooden pole has been burned to a stump and there's still some smoke coming from it.

'Tembelitsha School,' it says on the sign.

'Do you want me to stop here so you can get a picture?' asks my father.

My instinct is to say no, it's fine. But I want to get a closer look at the burning sign, and having my father with me makes it feel safer.

'OK,' I say.

There's a huddle of black men outside the shebeen. They look at me suspiciously when I get out the car with my camera, but they don't say or do anything. I feel uneasy. I get a quick shot of the sign and the broken bottles and get back in the car as soon as I can.

My father suggests we go to Elizabeth Koti's house, but he's not entirely sure where it is and neither am I, having been there only once before. I know it's next to the Ethembeni crèche, but I have no sense of direction, especially not in the squatter camps where the roads have no names. I point my father roughly towards where I think it might be and he drives the Jetta onto a dirt track that's so eroded, we might as well be off-road. I don't tell my father this, but

219

I'm impressed that he's brought me up here. This has always been my mother's territory in my mind.

We find Elizabeth's house eventually, after I convince my father to stop so we can ask an old lady for directions. The house looks fine; in fact, I'm a bit disappointed to see there's no sign that anything went on here at all.

'Maybe they didn't make it as far as this,' says my father. 'Johnny says the police were here.'

On the way out of Dam-se-Bos, we see two armoured riot vehicles on the other side of the N2, just sitting there. They remind me of the Casspirs that came to Knysna when I was little, except the Casspirs I remember were yellow, like the police vans used to be. These ones are white, like the police vans are now.

I didn't think the Casspirs were scary back then, maybe because their name sounded like the friendly ghost in my comic books. But seeing their modern-day equivalents now, they look like something from a dystopian future. Or rather, a dystopian past.

The following week there's an article about the riots in the *Herald*. Apparently the trouble started two nights before, on Wednesday, when people burned tyres and threw stones at cars in both Knysna and Plettenberg Bay. There's no mention of Elizabeth Koti personally, although the protestors in Knysna are identified as being from ward seven, Elizabeth's ward.

I'm glad I was nowhere near Dam-se-Bos on the night. According to the article, the protestors threw stones at cars on the N2 and even stoned a fire truck that was sent in to help. Police threw stun grenades and fired rubber bullets to break up the demonstration. It's scary to think that this was all happening just ten minutes from my parents' house, while we were probably watching soaps on TV.

I want to speak to Elizabeth, to find out how she's coping. But I don't call her, knowing it's surely the worst possible time. Instead, I read back over my notes from my last conversation with Elizabeth. It was nineteen months ago, in that same house I went to with my father this morning.

That day, Elizabeth told me about another riot in Knysna in the 1980s, when a child was shot dead by the police. 'Johnson Tatas', she called the boy, or just 'Tatas'. Elizabeth said he was the only casualty in Knysna during that time.

After I spoke to her, I scoured the Internet for information about the shooting, but found nothing. I was convinced there'd be at least something in the report from the Truth and Reconciliation Commission, or TRC. Set up by the ANC government, the TRC's aim was to give victims and perpetrators of apartheid atrocities the chance to talk about their experiences in a series of hearings. There were two types of hearing: human rights violation hearings where victims could tell their stories, and amnesty hearings for the police and other authorities who had been acting on orders from the apartheid government.

It was a chance for everyone to wipe the slate clean as we entered the New South Africa.

I find the Commission's full report online, but there are only six transcripts of hearings that refer to Knysna, mostly in passing. No mention of a Tatas or Johnson Tatas.

In the last transcript I read, I finally find a testimony about another child who got shot dead in Knysna. It says his name was Goodman Xokiso.

The child's mother testified at the hearing. But the transcript is confusing, not only because English obviously wasn't her first language – her testimony was no doubt translated from Xhosa or Afrikaans – but because the various descriptions of the event are so contradictory.

According to the transcript, police claimed the children were stoning a foot patrol and that was when the police opened fire, in self-defence. A lawyer, on the other hand, is quoted saying the police ambushed the children.

Then there's something about the child's funeral, how the mother and the community wanted him buried at the weekend but the police wouldn't allow it. But then the child was buried at the weekend anyway, with no one from the community present. And then the community turned on the mother and threatened her with violence . . . I lose track, as the mother's jumbled testimony makes it impossible to follow the story.

I doubt I'll ever find out what happened to Goodman Xokiso, not just because no one in Knysna seems to know who he was, but because of a paragraph towards the end of the TRC transcript, which quotes a Dr Ally:

> The Truth Commission has attempted to find out what has happened, but unfortunately . . . most of the documents have actually been destroyed . . . the case docket is not available [at the Knysna police station] and there are not hospital records that are available either.

With no police records or witnesses, I have nothing to go on.

Not until I find out by chance in one of my interviews that Goodman Xokiso and Johnson Tatas were the same person. And that his mother, Esther, is still alive and living in Flenterlokasie.

Chapter 37

Esther Xokiso

My mother takes me to Flenterlokasie. In the boot of the car there's a food parcel to say thank you to Esther Xokiso for seeing us. On my mother's recommendation, I've filled the parcel with staples that will keep without needing refrigeration, as Esther probably doesn't have electricity. My mother should know; she made up hundreds of similar parcels for black families during her time at Child Welfare.

In the box are packets of dried soup, instant coffee, tea bags, rice, fruit cordial, sugar, and some fresh fruit and vegetables – oranges, onions, bananas, butternut squash and apples. There's also a whole chicken that I took from the freezer just before we left the house. It won't stay frozen, but at least it'll be good for Esther's dinner tonight.

With no phone and no known address, Esther has been very hard to track down – even now, all I have is the name and number of a man who lives nearby.

That was how I set up today's meeting: by calling that man and asking him to go over to Esther's house to ask if

I could come and speak to her, then waiting for him to call me back to confirm.

My mother knows where the man lives, and that's where we park the car. Next to the house there's a building site with a tall hoarding around it.

'Oh no,' says my mother. 'That used to be the Red Church.'

We look at the hoarding, neither of us saying anything. We both know that, had the Red Church still been there, its walls would've been visible over the top of the hoarding; those corrugated iron walls painted red, the earthy terracotta of Klein Karoo dust. But we can't see anything over the top of the hoarding except the sky.

I know how much that building meant to my mother. It was where she started the first Flenterlokasie crèche with Paula Witney. It was where the Masakhane women got together every month to make their hats, handbags, mats and Wonder Boxes.

It was where my mother became Nobantu.

'That's so sad,' is all she says.

The man who helped set up the meeting with Esther comes out of his house and points out Esther's house down the hill. It isn't far, but the hill is steep and uneven. He lets us take a shortcut through his house, a nice single-storey brick building.

Esther's house, less than a hundred metres down the road, couldn't be more different.

Set back from the road with a dry patch of dirt in front of it, it's a shack in the truest sense of the word. It's made from narrow planks that look like they'll give way to age and gravity soon, and must barely be keeping out the elements in the meantime.

We find Esther in a small, dark room that I assume is a kitchen, only because there are saucepans and bowls on a shelf. But there's no fridge, cooker or a sink.

When I see Esther, I have to stop myself taking a step back. Her face is caked with some kind of red mud or paste that has dried into a cracked surface like a desert plain. Within that arid landscape, her eyes look like murky ponds.

Esther's appearance not only startles me, it frightens me. She reminds me of a witch doctor in a drama series about Shaka Zulu that gave me sleepless nights as a child. When I reach out to her, it's with the food parcel between us.

'This is for you,' I say.

She takes the food parcel from me.

'People said I was probably going to get money today, and now look at this,' she says in Afrikaans, taking the parcel from me. Her tone is jolly, but I get the sense she might have thought she was getting paid for the interview.

There's someone else in the room, a man about my age sitting with his back against the wall. She introduces him as her son, Headman.

My mother and I sit down near Headman on two hard seats, side by side.

Esther seems happy to talk, to the point of going off on tangents. But she makes the boundaries clear from the start. 'Just don't scratch,' she says, gesturing as if she's picking a scab off her head.

Esther tells us her children don't come to visit her. She says it's because she doesn't drink.

'The thing is, Nobantu,' she says to my mother, 'if you don't drink, the children don't want you.'

My mother nods politely. She doesn't drink either.

Headman is quiet and his face is hard to read. When he

does eventually speak, it's to correct his mother when she gets a fact wrong.

Esther treats him dismissively, as if his opinion doesn't count unless she has asked for it.

She had twelve children, Esther tells us, but only six of those have survived. Headman is the youngest one still alive.

I ask Esther how the six died and she remembers them one by one, counting them on her fingers. The first of her babies died the night it was born. The second one lived, then the third one died at around four years old. The fourth one died last April; she was a grown woman. And the rest all lived. Until Goodman was shot.

I've been counting along in my head and note that she's missed out a child, but I don't say anything.

Of her three remaining sons, one is in Cape Town and one is in prison, says Esther. Back when Goodman was shot, two of her sons were in prison.

'God put them there,' she says. 'To protect them when the toyi-toying started.'

I ask her what they were in prison for.

'I don't know, because as I say, it's the Lord who did it,' she says. 'A simple thing: go and break into the butchery just for *polony*. Then I said it was the Lord who did it, so that they could get away. Because if they'd been here, they'd have both been shot dead.'

She's talking about the riots.

I'm not sure whether she's saying her sons did actually break into a butchery to steal some processed meat, or whether she's just using it as an example of the kind of petty crime they might have committed. It's as ambiguous as the testimony she gave at the Truth and Reconciliation hearing.

I move on. How does she remember Goodman? What was he like as a child?

'Oh, he was a lamb,' she says, then becomes more guarded. 'I said not to scratch.'

I look at her face, trying to spot any kind of emotion, but it's hard to tell under all that flaking red paste.

'He was a soft child,' she says. 'If I told him off when he did something wrong, he'd say "Sorry, Mama." Not one of my other children, when they did something wrong, would come and say sorry. But he said, "Sorry, Mama."'

The boy was seventeen when he was shot. Esther says she warned him against going out to toyi-toyi. Headman interrupts to remind her that all the young people went out to toyi-toyi. They had to. If they didn't, they were threatened with necklacing – a form of punishment in the townships where a rubber tyre was flung over the condemned person's head, doused with petrol and set alight.

He speaks softly, mixing English and Afrikaans. 'If you don't go there, they come for you,' he says.

Despite the threats, Esther says she told Goodman not to go. 'And he said to me, "Mama, rather I die than you die."'

Because of that, Esther believes her son knew he was going to die that night. That he'd had a 'feeling'. She says she had a feeling, too.

When she heard the gunshot, she knew.

'I got a shock inside and I said, "That's my child."'

They only came to tell her the next morning, a priest and three women with blankets over their shoulders. Esther says she knew what they were coming to tell her. She told them to just come out and say it.

She didn't cry when they told her, she says. She didn't scream.

'I just made a sound like a dog when you scratch it.'

She makes the sound now, an awful, high-pitched moan that doesn't sound human. Wanting her to stop, or at least wanting an excuse to look away, I turn my attention to Headman. How did he feel when he found out his brother was dead?

'*Yoh*, I screamed,' he says. 'I loved my brother very much.' Where there was no emotion in his eyes before, there are tears now.

Headman says he was thirteen when his brother was shot. He wasn't there himself on the night, but he heard the stories of what had happened. He relays those stories as if they're undisputed facts, but I know from what I've read that there are many versions of the night's events.

In Headman's version, the children were hiding from the police. But there was a black man with the police who called to the children in Xhosa, saying it was safe to come out. When the children did, the police started shooting.

I ask him whether that means the police ambushed the children, as the lawyer later claimed at the TRC hearing.

'Yes. It was a trap,' he says.

After Goodman's death, there was to be a memorial service at Esther's house every night until the funeral, as was the Xhosa way. But, Esther says, the nightly gatherings became an extension of the toyi-toying and demonstrations. When the police turned up, there was a lot of cursing and shouting, the police calling the black people 'Mandela's dogs'.

My mother cuts in to explain to me that, in Xhosa culture, 'dog' is one of the most offensive things you can call someone.

I move on to the funeral. What happened? Why was it so controversial?

Esther's explanation now is just as confusing as her official

228

testimony. She uses 'week' and 'weekend' interchangeably, so that I have to keep asking her to clarify what she means until I'm satisfied I'm following her.

According to Esther, she wanted to bury her son at the weekend so that all her children could come to the funeral, and maybe bring their church congregations with them.

The black community also wanted it to be at the weekend, but for a different reason. They wanted to give the boy a 'comrade's funeral', which meant bussing people in from the surrounding areas and turning it into a public event with speeches and singing and toyi-toying.

If the comrades had their way, the funeral would culminate in a procession through the streets of Knysna to the municipal cemetery, with the boy's coffin carried aloft all the way.

Esther didn't want more blood shed in her child's name. Nor did the police, who picked her up from her house and took her to the police station to convince her in secret to bury Goodman on a weekday. When she refused, they threatened to have the boy buried by *bandiete* – prisoners – if she didn't comply.

In the end they came to a compromise. Esther could bury her son on a Saturday, as long as she didn't tell anyone except her closest family.

By the time it came to the funeral, Goodman's body had been in the morgue for more than a month and a half.

Esther took just five people with her that Saturday – two daughters and three of their friends. The only other people there were the police and a coloured minister.

'It wasn't even a funeral,' she says. 'That's what hurts me. My child was buried like a dog. Because when you bury a dog, there's no prayer.'

229

The black community's antagonism against her is starting to make sense to me. They must have felt she'd robbed them of the biggest opportunity to show their anger to the world. Or worse, that she was in cahoots with the police.

I ask Esther about a story that went round the community, that she sold Goodman's body to the police.

Her mood changes immediately and she reacts almost violently, spitting on the floor, hard. She wipes her mouth and there's raw rage in her eyes.

'There was a story like that,' she says, her voice louder now. 'To defile my name because I took the child without speaking to them. That's why they said I sold the body to the police. I heard it with my own ears.'

She says the community became so antagonistic towards her that she fled Flenterlokasie for a month until things died down.

My mother has been listening intently, nodding and hmm–ing in all the right places. She's been particularly good at helping Headman be heard, insisting that Esther should let him speak when he's had something to say.

But now my mother is frowning. She leans forward in her seat. 'What I can't understand is this,' she says. 'He should have been like a hero. He died for the struggle they were fighting for. So he should have been an example for all the children. But instead they were mad at you. I don't understand how that adds up.'

Esther has an answer. 'The thing is,' she says, 'we who are the child's family, we don't fight with them.'

My mother sits back again, her frown gone.

'Oh, OK,' she says gently. 'I understand now. It was only Goodman who went to toyi-toyi. Of all your children, it was only him.'

Esther nods.

But, she says, everything's fine now. The community aren't treating her badly. And as for Goodman's death, she's made peace with it.

'I say thank you that the Lord has taken him,' she says. 'He doesn't have sin before the Lord. And that thing he said, "Mama, rather I die . . ." He took my place. Some people say when you're seventy you must go, die. But here I am, still living. Maybe because he said those words.'

And the police? How does she feel towards them after everything that happened?

'Oh, I can't blame anyone,' says Esther. 'Because it was like that everywhere. If it only happened here in Knysna, then I could still understand it. But all around us it was like that, even now, it's still a fight. People are still toyi-toying, maybe the white man won't pay, or give them a raise, then they toyi-toyi.'

I think of the burning tyres in Dam-se-Bos just the other day.

The conversation moves on to money again, my mother saying she might be able to help Esther with a municipal grant to improve her house. She just needs Esther's identity book, which Esther promptly produces from between her large breasts.

Like all South Africans, I have a similar ID book. The size and shape of a passport, it has a laminated page for your personal details, including your unique identification number, which you spend your life quoting on official documents, forms and phone calls. The rest of the book used to be for things like driving and firearm licences, although newer driving licences come in a more practical card format.

My mother compliments Esther on the picture in her ID

book, suggesting her beauty might be from the 'make-up'. I spot the chance to ask her what she's got on her face.

'Avocado stone,' she says. To protect her skin.

Before we go, I ask Headman if there's anyone else I can talk to; anyone who might have been there the night Goodman was shot.

'There is a guy who works at the municipality,' he says. 'Zola Plaatjies.'

In Zola's version of the story, told over a coffee at the Mugg and Bean in town, there were over a hundred, maybe two hundred people outside the Tembelitsha School. They dragged desks into the road, even trees from the forest that they'd cut down using chainsaws. Anything they could use as obstacles for the 'hippos' to drive over. That's what they called the Casspirs, with their snout-like grilles.

They threw stones at the police vans, and petrol bombs. When some of the petrol bombs didn't explode, they went back to stones.

The children hid from the police, until someone called that it was safe to come out. *Bamkile*, they shouted. 'They have left.' Whoever it was who shouted that the coast was clear, the children believed them. The police vans were gone, and so were the Casspirs.

But the police were still there.

When the children came out of hiding, the police started shooting.

I believe that Zola's version of events is as true as anyone's memories from twenty-three years ago can be. But if there's one thing I've come to realise in my time here, it's that there's more than one side to every story.

Chapter 38

1986

When Owéna heard the news at Child Welfare that a child had been shot, she didn't press the messenger for details. She didn't want to know. It was all getting very political. And the line between her job and politics was one she wasn't willing to cross.

Despite the death of the child, the situation in Knysna wasn't nearly as bad as in other parts of South Africa. For months, children had been rising up at schools all over the country. And it wasn't just happening in faraway places like Johannesburg or Cape Town. Some of the most violent reports came from Oudtshoorn, a hundred and twenty kilometres from Knysna, where police were shooting and arresting protesting schoolchildren.

But while children elsewhere were burning their classrooms, the Tembelitsha principal in Knysna had been building new ones at his school just months before.

Owéna was pleased to hear that the same principal, Mr Hewana, had stopped his school choir from entering a singing competition in Oudtshoorn, knowing they risked being indoctrinated by their more militant and aggressive peers.

But Mr Hewana couldn't shield the children from everything.

Owéna saw it on the news and in the papers. In towns and cities across South Africa, black people were coming together and standing up for their rights.

The Eastern Cape had become one of the country's most politically charged areas, with ongoing workers' strikes and consumer boycotts crippling its economy. Black people who didn't observe the strikes and boycotts were punished by their own people. It was the Eastern Cape that gave rise to necklacing, the cruellest of those punishments.

A brutal form of lynching, necklacing was usually reserved for those exposed as *impimpies* – police informers. The community watched as the person burned, suffocating from the smoke bellowing from the tyre around their neck.

There hadn't been any necklacings in Knysna, but the local community punished its people in other ways. During a boycott of the shops in town, anyone caught with groceries bought anywhere but from the black-owned *spaza* or squatter-camp shops was made to eat or drink their purchases – whether it was bleach or washing powder, cooking oil or raw chicken.

Being caught under the influence was just as serious an offence, as alcohol was only available in town. Owéna heard at least one story of a man who was lashed with a *sjambok* for being drunk.

The police didn't do much. And nor could Owéna.

As a social worker, she couldn't be seen to take sides. She hadn't even voted in the previous general election, knowing that any political affiliation could break down the trust she'd worked so long to build up among the black people. For the same reason, she couldn't be seen to side with, or even work with, the police when the unrest started.

But nor did she want to join the black people's struggle. Being associated with any kind of militant action would go against the very principles of her work.

All she could do was watch as the violence got worse, and help the families affected in the aftermath.

Chapter 39

David Ngxale

My next interview is with David Ngxale, a man I'm hoping can give me another angle on the Goodman Xokiso story, as I've been told he was a youth leader in the black community back then.

I find him at the Black Sash offices, where he works.

Founded in the 1950s, the Black Sash started out as a women's resistance organisation that spoke out against racial inequality. It was named after the signature black sashes worn by its members – both white women and black – during public demonstrations.

Since the end of apartheid, the organisation has shifted its focus from racial inequality to more practical, day-to-day assistance for people in need.

As a paralegal advisor at the Black Sash, David Ngxale helps people with things like labour issues, social security, pensions and state grants.

The first thing that strikes me about him is how soft-spoken he is. He barely looks at me when we speak, focusing on his desk or looking over my shoulder instead.

David tells me he was born in 1959 but he looks older than fifty, maybe because he has no teeth. I can't imagine this quiet, toothless man in front of me rallying thousands of people with an impassioned speech.

His shyness makes me doubt whether he's the best person to speak to. But, I reason to myself, while I'm here, I might as well hear his story.

David tells me he was part of the Knysna Youth Organisation in the 1980s. I've not heard of it before. He says it set out to 'educate people politically'.

Born in Knysna, David was raised to be politically conscious. His father, having grown up in the Eastern Cape and been involved in the unrest there, knew more than most about what was going on in the rest of the country. He shared that information with his son from an early age.

When David went to the Eastern Cape himself, first to school and then to university, he got to see the struggle first-hand: the industrial action, the protests, the strength in numbers. But he also saw another side to the struggle: the charred remains of *impimpies* who'd been necklaced by their communities, and the police who laughed when they found those bodies the next morning.

It was when he came back to Knysna in December 1985 that David got involved in the 'political education' of the local people. He told them what was happening around South Africa; that people were starting to stand up against apartheid.

It wasn't long before he was arrested.

'I was the first person to be picked up,' he says, 'because they said I was the one who instigated the unrest in the area.'

I ask him what sorts of things happened during the unrest.

'There was stone-throwing, and there was also a bus that was set alight,' he says. 'And one person was shot to death.'

He's talking about Goodman, of course. But like everyone besides Esther and Headman Xokiso, he refers to him as Tatas.

David says he was arrested shortly after the shooting, but the dates don't add up. David is convinced it was February 1986, but I know the Truth and Reconciliation transcript says the shooting was in March.

When I point this out, David questions the validity of the testimony. He's critical of the TRC, saying it took whatever individuals were saying as the truth, with no one to challenge their testimonies. But he does confirm the story that people accused Esther of selling her son's body to the apartheid government.

David says he has met Esther since then. In his role as paralegal advisor, he helped her get a special pension – a pay-out given to relatives of people who died during the struggle.

We get back to David's arrests, as it turns out there were more than one. He says the time after Tatas's death, he was arrested for public violence. Another time the charge was illegal gathering. In both cases, he claims he wasn't even present at the gatherings in question; that he was arrested only for being seen as a leader and an instigator.

Young people who were being arrested gave him up to the police, he says. The ones who didn't have any experience of being arrested for things like public violence. He claims it was common practice for police to make detainees give them names – or confirm the names they already had – in return for their release.

But he holds no grudges against the people who gave him up.

'They were still young,' he says. 'And they wanted to go home.'

After being released on bail for the second time in 1986, he was finally arrested under the national state of emergency. But whereas most of the other detainees were sent to George, David was kept in Knysna, in a separate cell.

'They didn't want me to mix with the others,' he says.

So they really thought he was the big instigator?

'*Ja*,' he says.

Would he say he was?

He laughs, a shy, quiet laugh.

'No,' he says softly. 'No.'

He's quiet for the longest time. He has the saddest eyes I've ever seen.

Eventually it's me who breaks the silence.

'How did the police treat you?'

'I was tortured,' he says. 'I was the worst person tortured in the Knysna police station.'

I'm not prepared for David's answer and it throws me off-guard.

He mumbles something about going to the TRC to testify, but I've stopped listening. My brain is groping around in the dark, trying to find a light switch. David Ngxale. David Ngxale. I don't remember seeing the name in the TRC transcripts, but I haven't looked at any except Goodman Xokiso's for a while.

Still, I would've remembered something as serious as torture.

The list of questions I prepared last night isn't going to help me now. I ask the first question that comes to mind.

'What did they do to you?'

'Assaulted me,' he says. 'Handcuffed while I'm being assaulted. And I have been put in that tube.' He uses his hands to mime a cylindrical object sliding tightly over his head.

He tries to explain it, a tube he says they used in 'the olden days' to close a person's mouth, their nose and their ears so they couldn't breathe.

The police shocked him too, he says. They put something on his fingers and shocked him.

David says the torture was intended to make him admit he was the person leading the whole unrest, that he was part of a committee working beyond Knysna in Oudtshoorn, Mossel Bay and George. He *was* on that committee, he tells me now. But he wouldn't admit it then. Because, he says, they could force you to make a statement saying that whatever happened, you were part of it. And if you were then found guilty, you could be sent to prison for years.

I look at David and wonder how the police could do those things to this man who seems so gentle. Yet surely he would've had to be a different person then to play such a big part in the unrest. To make people listen to him.

He insists he wasn't inciting violence; that, if anything, he was telling the children to stop throwing stones at police. His work was more about planning activities in the area, and showing people how they could demonstrate to the government that the people of the Southern Cape weren't satisfied with the apartheid system.

Violence, he says, was a different thing. When leaders were absent, people could take decisions and 'just do things'.

So does he think that's where the violence came from?

That, when the leaders were detained, there was no one to keep the people back?

He thinks about it for a long while, as if it's never occurred to him before. Then he says: 'That's correct.'

I wonder whether David was involved in the intimidation, remembering Headman's story about the youth being threatened if they didn't join in the toyi-toying. I ask David if it's true.

'No,' he says. 'Only when you make bad remarks and someone hears you, then that someone will take you to the community. Then you will be called.'

An example of a bad remark, he says, would be something like 'I won't involve myself with those people.' So basically any kind of dissent, by the sound of it, much like Headman had told me and my mother.

'It was better to keep quiet,' he says. 'If you don't want to get punished, keep quiet and do your things and don't make any remarks.'

I tell him people should have a right to voice their opinions and he agrees, but he says there were meetings for that. The problem was that some people were speaking their minds away from those meetings, discouraging others from joining the struggle.

I want to know more, but our time is up.

In the car I curse and bang my hands on the steering wheel. How could I have missed something this big in the TRC reports? David told me he'd gone to the commission to testify about the torture, so there must be a record of the hearing.

I go to an Internet cafe, where I google David's name. But besides a team picture on the Black Sash website, there's nothing.

I read and reread all six TRC reports that mention Knysna, but find no mention of David.

Only later, when I'm transcribing the interview, do I realise that I misheard him. When I thought he said he *had* gone to the Truth and Reconciliation Commission, he actually said he *hadn't*. The rest of our conversation makes more sense now, when David said he didn't want to be reminded of what had happened.

David also said he's since met the people who tortured and assaulted him – that he's even friends with one of them now. He said he buys things from the man's farm sometimes; that he gets meat at cheap prices.

I ask my father if there are any ex-policemen who are farming in the area.

'Just the one,' he says. 'Nice guy.'

I have no trouble finding the man's number in the phone book. But before I call him, I know I need to speak to David again first. He never gave me the policeman's name, and it would be wrong to go behind his back. I also want to find out more about his relationship with the policeman, hoping for a real feel-good story of reconciliation.

So I'm disappointed when David tells me there was no dramatic confrontation or teary reconciliation. He says they just started greeting each other on the street.

I ask him if he'd be willing to give me the man's name. He does, and it's the same name my father gave me. David says it's OK for me to call the man, even for me to tell him we've spoken. He doesn't have his phone number, though.

I don't tell him I've already got it, just that I'm sure I can find it.

Chapter 40

Lawrence Oliver

When I call Lawrence Oliver and explain that I want to speak to him about a book I'm writing, he sounds suspicious at first. But when I tell him I'm looking specifically into the unrest of 1986, he eases up.

'I investigated all of those cases,' he says, and agrees to see me on his farm.

I don't mention David Ngxale, worried that Lawrence will change his mind if I do.

Until now, I've only managed to track down one other retired policeman who was far less forthcoming when I went to his house.

I arrived unannounced and, even after I explained who my parents were, the policeman was cagey. He refused to talk about the time of the unrest, saying simply that it was behind him and he didn't want to go there.

He didn't reckon anyone else would help me either. The 'normal' policemen were just on patrol, he said. Anything that happened 'behind the curtain', they wouldn't know about.

And he said no one would tell me what they did personally.

Before I left, he had a question for me.

'What do you want from this?'

'Just the truth,' I replied.

He gave a cynical little laugh.

'You'll never find the truth,' he said.

Lawrence Oliver is a big man with the kind of downturned eyes that make him look permanently sad. When he comes to meet me at the car, he's dressed like your typical South African farmer, in shorts and a short-sleeve button shirt. He's holding back two big, excitable dogs.

Lawrence leads me into his living room where there's a black woman vacuuming noisily. Or maybe she's coloured; I know now that you can't assume. He asks her to stop and do something else for now, and she disappears towards the back of the house.

I sit down at a large dining table while he fetches us some water.

If I was worried that Lawrence wasn't going to talk, I needn't have been. Once he gets going, it seems he'll never stop. Although I have many questions to get through, I let him talk, all too aware that this might be my only chance to hear the police's side of the story.

Lawrence says he came to Knysna as a police constable in 1983. Before that, he was in Soweto. He's clearly still haunted by the memories of his time in South Africa's most notorious township. As he goes back there now, those downturned eyes look even sadder. Forty-six policemen were murdered while he was in Soweto, he says. In comparison, Knysna was peaceful. Until suddenly it started 'flaring up' here as well.

He tells one story after another of what it was like when

the unrest started in Knysna. How the police always had to be alert because they never knew when the next riot was going to start. How white people's cars were stoned indiscriminately – an old man going to church, a young couple on honeymoon, innocent people who were just on the wrong road at the wrong time. And you could never help the first ones, he says. Once it started, you could block the roads and divert traffic. But you could never help the first ones.

He tells me how black policemen's houses were set alight by their communities, how he went to those houses to get the policemen's children out before they burned to death.

He remembers one particular night when he was driving up to the black areas to get someone out and the road was blocked with burning tables from the Tembelitsha School, and he had to stop the van and they came, they just came with their petrol bombs and their stones . . .

I ask him how that felt.

'I still get . . .' He rubs his arms to indicate goose bumps. 'It's crazy . . .'

He goes very quiet.

'Did any of the policemen get hurt?' I ask.

'Not that night, because . . .'

He stops again.

'I can't do this,' he says, looking at the table, avoiding my eyes.

He takes a sip of water, pulls himself together. He takes a deep breath.

'Not that night,' he says again.

Of all the things he saw, he says what the black people did to each other was often the worst, how they intimidated and punished each other. Maybe that was their success, he says. That they kept everyone in line.

He's quick to add that a lot of people were willing and loyal. But he reckons many were also joining in through fear. And that's not right.

Throughout our conversation, he keeps coming back to honesty, fairness and doing what's right. They're clearly principles he values very highly.

'I'm a funny *oke*,' he says. A funny guy. 'If a thing's right, it's right. If it's wrong, it's wrong.'

It's because of the truth that he left the police in the late 1990s. He calls to his wife to bring over a newspaper clipping and while she's looking for it, he tells me the story.

Years ago, Lawrence says, a Knysna woman was assaulted and almost killed by a man who was on bail on a rape charge. Not long before the attack, that same woman had reported the man to the police after spotting him watching her through the window of her house. At the time she asked the police to re-arrest the man, but they did nothing.

After the attack, the woman brought a case against the state for failing to protect her. But when it went to court, the prosecutors denied that anything had ever been brought to the attention of the police.

Lawrence knew they were lying, because he'd been on duty when the woman came to report the man's suspicious behaviour. And so he agreed to testify against the state.

Shortly before the trial, Lawrence was visited by two men from the attorney-general's office, wanting to know what his intentions were. He said he was giving evidence because the woman was telling the truth.

'Just remember who you work for,' they said.

He went ahead and testified regardless.

Almost immediately afterwards, he was told he was being

transferred to the Khayalitsha township in Cape Town. He resigned there and then.

Lawrence's wife has found the newspaper clipping.

'Detective in Knysna attack case resigns for "the truth",' says the headline next to a picture of Lawrence.

I wonder if he might give me the truth that his ex-colleague said I'd never find.

I steer the conversation back to the unrest of 1986 and soon Lawrence is recalling a story of being in a Casspir in Witlokasie and having to drive over a flaming car in the road. The Casspir got stuck on the car and the flames came up the side and he thought he was done for.

And yet he expresses empathy with the rioters, acknowledging that they did what they did to protect their children and their future and their lives.

'I say to myself if I was in that position, I'd probably have done the same thing,' he says. 'Maybe us whites are going to be in that position . . . Who knows.'

It's a cynical view of the current situation in South Africa, and one that I know he shares with many white people in the country.

What really got to him back then, says Lawrence, was the way small children were used in the struggle. It's a point he keeps coming back to, likening it to similar techniques used in Palestine and Israel, Iraq and Iran.

He says there were children no older than eight or ten who were made to go and join the marches. Adults used them like pawns, because they knew if a child got shot, it would reflect badly on the police.

It's a different story with seventeen, eighteen year olds, he says. They can think for themselves.

I'm reminded of Tatas and ask him about the shooting.

'I was there that night,' he says, sitting back in his chair. 'I've been in the court a thousand times for that now.'

I can't believe my luck.

In Lawrence's version of the story, there was no ambush, nor were there any Xhosas with them. They were just five or six policemen, defending themselves against a violent crowd.

He says the children were burning tables from the Tembelitsha School in the road and he and his colleagues went up there to clear it up. The children started throwing stones at them. They ordered the children to stop and they didn't. So the children got shot. But it's impossible to know which one of those five or six policemen fired the shot that killed the boy.

'It went through an inquest, it went through a court case, it went through the Supreme Court,' he says, 'and right through till the end it was found to be a legal shooting. And that was years apart, each one . . . And it was the same outcome.'

He explains that it's the same law today as it was then: if you're being attacked and you suspect your life's in imminent danger, you can shoot.

He says many of those children would have been arrested for public violence, one of the main charges during that time along with illegal gatherings, intimidation, riotous behaviour and sabotage.

I'm surprised to hear of incidents of sabotage in Knysna, of telephone lines being cut and a sawmill set alight. I've heard stories of how the ANC used to blow up things like electricity pylons, but I thought that only happened in the big cities.

I ask him what he reckons the most serious thing was that the police managed to prevent.

'Them getting into town,' he says.

He tells me how the police held back crowds of maybe a thousand people gathered in the road that runs from Witlokasie to the centre of Knysna.

'I can't even imagine what they would've done if they got into the middle of town,' he says.

It could easily have happened, by the sound of it. Lawrence says the police were struggling to cope. Knysna simply didn't have enough officers – 'if there were forty-eight of us it was a lot' – and there was no support or back-up from the surrounding towns, where they were having similar problems of their own. The only riot squad in the area was in Oudtshoorn, where they had their hands full with especially violent protests.

Lawrence paints a grim picture of what it was like being a policeman at the time: the relentless shifts of twelve hours on, twelve hours off; constantly having to be on standby in case the violence flared up; the not knowing when it would; the fear when it did.

As the police were slowly getting worn down, he says the state of emergency was necessary – even though he can see how the emergency regulations might have looked bad 'to the law people'.

'When you're in it yourself, when you've got to manage a station or a town, and you've got to protect the people of the town, and you've only got X amount of people,' he says, 'then those laws had to be in effect.'

If they hadn't been, he says, 'things could have gone terribly sour.'

'I think a lot of white people in this country would have

realised what's really going on,' he says. 'I mean, they would have felt the wrath of it.'

Having spoken to several of those white people in Knysna, I've come to realise most of them genuinely didn't know what was going on.

'They didn't have a clue,' he says. 'You know one day we came down in the Casspir and they had just burned houses up there and I was standing in the top of the Casspir and we came down the main road . . . And people were walking around on holiday, in shorts with bikinis on, and I just looked and I thought fuck, don't these people know what's going on? We turned around maybe a thousand people that were coming to town to cause havoc. And here they're walking in bikinis. I thought, Christ, don't these people know what's going on in this country? It was like two flippin' worlds.'

As part of the national state of emergency, police could arrest and detain people for months without trial. Lawrence says it was a way of removing the leaders; the people who were stirring the violence in each town.

And yet he says he's friends with some of those people now, as he was before the unrest. One of them, he says, calls him his 'white son'. I know the man he's talking about; he's a prominent figure in the township who was detained in 1986, as was his wife.

Lawrence compares it with a rugby match.

'It's like if the Australians and the South Africans play, and they've been touring together . . . When you're on the field, you go for each other and afterwards it's like, "Let's go and have a beer, mate. Good tackle." It's very much simplifying what it was like, but in a lot of the cases it was like that.'

Of his black friend, he says, 'He knew that I had to do what I had to do, and he had to stand by what he had to do.'

But there was a difference between what the police 'had' to do, and what they could choose not to do. Lawrence says a lot of people now say they couldn't refuse to do something because they'd be disobeying an order. But if that order were to murder or assassinate a man, as certain members of the security police were told to do, it would be illegal.

'It's like warfare. Like Guantanamo Bay,' he says. 'Obviously they're torturing those people to interrogate them. That happens in all warfare. I mean, I always say it's so unfair to sit outside of a war or a situation and try and think or portray how people must think and do and act . . . If you've got people trying to kill you and you're trying to kill them, and now you happen to capture one of them . . . You are in warfare or, call it what you want, there is a sense of fear on both sides . . . And people did a lot of things that they shouldn't have done, but again, it's in the context of that warfare, of that time. It's not sitting months down the line or years down the line and trying to debate and say, "But that wasn't quite nice what you did to that chap."'

I realise this is the perfect opportunity to bring up David Ngxale, but I don't. I'm worried Lawrence will stop talking if I do, and there's another question I want to ask first.

'Did you ever think you were going to die?'

'Often. Very often.'

But, he says, the police were conditioned to think of death; to be aware of their own mortality. He tells me how, on riot training, they were shown videos of black people being necklaced and policemen being killed, much like my father said he'd seen the Angola soldiers being trained in a documentary. One video, says Lawrence, showed an over-turned police van in the township being attacked by a crowd of people who pulled the bars off the windows, pulled the policemen out and 'literally chopped them up'.

Another video, he says, went round a mortuary, round and round a mortuary full of murdered policemen and you could just about make out the remains and the badge on the one guy's shirt, and his head was cut open and the video just went round and round.

'And it sort of gets in your mind,' he says. '"Whatever I do, I must make sure that never happens to me."'

I go back to his point about Guantanamo Bay; that people knew 'things were going on'. I can't bring myself to use the word 'torture', so I ask: 'Was there stuff going on in Knysna?'

Uh-uh, he says, no. Then: 'Investigating normal murders, like that little schoolgirl who was raped and murdered in Knysna . . . That's another thing. Political investigations were harder. A lot harder.'

He's been referring to the unrest as 'political' all along, to differentiate it from what his actual area of expertise had been: investigating rapes and murders. The little girl he's referring to was an especially high-profile case years ago. Everyone in Knysna knew about it.

I get the feeling he didn't particularly want to get involved in the 'political stuff', but he had no choice.

The reason the political investigations were harder, he says, was because the police were constantly watched by attorneys and human rights organisations like the Black Sash. Even during the state of emergency, whenever someone was arrested, a doctor had to come and examine them, and again when they were released. Ever since Steve Biko 'died from his questioning'.

Biko was an anti-apartheid activist who died in 1977 after being tortured during a police interrogation in Port Elizabeth.

That's where the emergency regulations helped, he says. Because the detentions without trial gave the police the time they needed to question the suspects – unlike other crimes where they only got forty-eight hours to either release or prosecute. So if people wouldn't talk, they just stayed in prison until they did.

He tells me how those emergency regulations were particularly useful in riot cases where there wasn't just one accused, and cases like the burning of the sawmill where there might have been thirty or forty people involved. In a case like that, forty-eight hours simply wouldn't have been enough to get to the bottom of it.

And again, he says, it gave the police the opportunity to go for the leaders.

But there wasn't just one leader either, Lawrence says. The police were trying to remove entire 'cells' of people.

In a few of my interviews, people have referred to 'the list'; some kind of hit list with the names of all the leaders the police were tasked with arresting immediately after the state of emergency was announced.

Lawrence confirms that there was such a list. It came from the security police.

I see my chance and I take it.

'I spoke to a guy the other day who thinks he was top of the hit list. A guy called David Ngxale.'

I'm expecting Lawrence to agree, to say yes, David was a leader, maybe to add what a nice guy he actually is and that they're friends now. But he doesn't say any of that.

'David Ngxale, *ag* please, man,' he says, pulling a disgusted face. 'You know, I call him a wannabe . . . I think the government paid him out. I think ten thousand rand, for a slap he got.'

I haven't mentioned anything about the alleged assault or torture, but we've certainly moved on to the assault. That David might have got a pay-out is news to me.

Lawrence clearly has no time for David, and has no reservations about telling me exactly why.

'He was a stirrer,' he says. 'He was the main one, all the kids will tell you that he would sweep them up to come and join the little protests.'

Those kids, says Lawrence, were young – little ones of about seven, eight, nine, ten years old. He says David told those children not to go to school some days; that they had to come and join the protests instead. He says the kids he spoke to were terrified of David, that they didn't want to go and march but David made them, threatening and intimidating them.

I come right out and say it.

'David is saying that while he was in jail in Knysna, he was tortured.'

Lawrence responds without any hesitation. 'He was *moered*, ja. I think he was,' he says, using a crass Afrikaans word for 'beaten up'. 'But I think the government paid him out for that . . . I think he went to Supreme Court for somebody slapping him somewhere or in the charge office or something.'

I bring up the 'tube' that David said was put over his face, and the electric shock. Lawrence denies it, saying he's seen that kind of thing on TV but, 'Uh-uh, not him.'

So he doesn't think that kind of thing happened here?

'Not with political stuff,' he says.

When I ask him whether he ever questioned David, he launches into another diatribe about how he doesn't like

David because he got those kids involved who shouldn't have been involved. And yet, in the middle of it all, he acknowledges that it might have been David's 'job' to do that; that he might have been instructed to round up the children.

Either way, for Lawrence it comes back to how the children were being used.

He refers to it as 'warfare' again, but points out that it's warfare in a civilian situation which makes it awkward because you don't just have two sides going for each other 'like a boxing match.' Instead, he says, it's 'like having a boxing match in a preschool. A kid can get hurt.'

I remember David's eyes and ask the one question that's going round and round in my mind:

'So why would he lie to me and say he was tortured?'

Lawrence sits back in his chair.

'He's not necessarily lying to you.'

I get bolder. 'So do you think that stuff could have happened?'

'It could have,' he says. 'Very possible. I know he was slapped . . . I can't remember who slapped him, it could've been me, I don't even know. But it was because we had been questioning about thirty kids and they were all terrified of him and said he was the one who made them do it, and the way he threatened them . . .'

Lawrence says it didn't help that David 'had an attitude' when the police picked him up.

But still, he denies that there were any electric shocks, saying that 'even your own bosses would hang you up' if you did something like that. When I press him, he finally admits that kind of thing did happen, but that it was more the security police who did it.

He asks me where David claims all of this happened. Caught off guard, I say 'in the cells'. The truth is, David didn't stipulate.

But it's too late. Lawrence goes on to explain at length how it couldn't have happened in a cell; that there was no electricity supply – unless you used the lights – and that the cells were visited regularly.

'If you want to question somebody, you book them out of the cells and you take them to your office or to wherever,' he says. 'To do that in the cells and you know there are attorneys walking around or the Black Sash people walking around, you've got to be bloody stupid.'

In case it wasn't clear before, I tell Lawrence that David Ngxale 'kind of implicated' him in the whole thing.

'Oh he would, *ja*,' says Lawrence, sounding unsurprised.

He vehemently disagrees with David's claims that they're friends now. 'I don't like him. That's as simple as it is,' he says. 'But then, in hindsight, whatever he says I did, shocked him or whatever . . . Why didn't I do it to the rest of them? Why him?'

When I suggest it might be because David says he was at the top of the list, Lawrence reiterates his point that, as far as he's concerned, David was 'just a small part of the whole puzzle', and 'just a little boy'.

Then he adds: 'But it's the way he threatened the kids.'

He draws another analogy, this time comparing the situation with arresting a child molester.

'If you're speaking to a little girl that's been molested, and she says my stepfather does this and this to me . . . You see that kid and you think *jis*, that's sick. When you go and fetch that guy, you don't go to him and say, "Sir, please come with us." And if he starts getting aggressive with you,

256

you don't need much to want to sort of push him a bit harder into the car than you would've another person.'

He reminds me that he used to investigate murders, even serial killings. He's seen some gruesome things. And he admits to having had a reputation among the criminals for doing everything from threatening to push someone off the Heads to drowning a man in the sea, 'with steel, like the mafia do'.

He used that reputation to his advantage, he says. It helped to get people to talk.

I ask him if all the stories were made up.

'Not all of them,' he says. 'But most of them.'

He tells me about one case where a man had been robbing people regularly and threatening them with a gun. When Lawrence confronted him, he refused to hand over the gun. So Lawrence questioned him. And he got the gun.

'If you're a good detective, sometimes you have to question people. People who tell you you don't, they lie.'

I've suspected for a while that he's using the word 'questioning' as a euphemism for something more persuasive, ever since he said Steve Biko died 'from questioning'. This time I ask him outright what he means by it.

'*Ag*, whether you threaten them or slap them or drown them . . . Dunk his head in the bath, or whatever you've got to do to get him to talk. Now from the outside it looks terrible . . . But from the inside, you've got to do your job. It's as simple as that.'

But there came a time, says Lawrence, when he started feeling less and less comfortable with that side of the job. The incident with the man and the gun became a kind of turning point for him.

The problem he had, he says, was that the detectives

would pray every morning, asking God to be with them. And for the first time, he stopped to think about what that really meant: that God was watching them.

He started feeling very uncomfortable with the idea of God seeing him 'question' people.

So he went to different ministers and theologians for their opinions. One minister told him that God knew there had to be policemen and that they had to do things like that, as long as he wasn't doing it for self-satisfaction. Another said he should pray for the man to give him the gun and if the man didn't and killed someone, then it was God's will.

Neither of those answers satisfied Lawrence.

Then a third minister said: 'If it worries you, get out of that job.'

So he did.

He gave up being a detective and went 'back to uniform' where he would happily take a statement when there'd been a murder, but even more happily give that statement to a detective to get to the truth.

'How he gets to the truth is his problem,' he says. 'It's not my problem.'

But, he adds, it was 'a coward's way out'.

He stayed in uniform until the day he resigned.

If he had to go back and do it all over again, he'd still interrogate murderers, he says. If it stopped them raping and killing little girls.

Before I leave, I tell Lawrence about the only other ex-policeman I've managed to see, the one who told me I wouldn't find the truth.

'Oh no, you won't get the truth,' he says, claiming that policemen from that time are scared to speak out after some of them were locked up instead of getting amnesty from the Truth and Reconciliation Commission.

'Have you been telling me the truth today?' I ask him.

He thinks for a while.

'Ninety-nine point nine percent,' he says.

On the way home, I replay David and Lawrence's contradicting stories in my mind. I don't know what to believe any more. David was almost certainly beaten by the police. But was he tortured? And where do you draw the line?

I share my dilemma on Twitter: who do I believe, ex-cop or alleged victim?

A South African friend in London replies: 'Ex-cop under-played it, victim exaggerated it. Both told you the truth they remember: the one that makes them more right.'

It might be the closest I'm going to get to the truth: the reminder that there's more than one side to it.

Even the Truth and Reconciliation Commission seems to support this argument. In volume six, section three, chapter one of the Commission's official report, I find a section headed 'Torture and assault'.

This is what it says:

The Amnesty Committee received applications specifying only ninety cases of torture or assault . . . These figures stand in sharp contrast to the 4,792 torture violations recorded in [human rights violation] statements. These low figures may be partly explained by the fact that perpetrators seldom seem to have regarded torture as a major violation.

259

Chapter 41

1986

When news spread of 'the list', many of Knysna's black children took on a new, nomadic lifestyle.

Police had started raiding their homes, looking for those children who were regularly spotted among the toyi-toying crowds. The raids usually happened at night, police moving from one shack to the next to pick up the 'troublemakers'.

The children got crafty, never staying in one place for long. Sometimes they spent the night with friends they knew weren't being targeted, in rooms with separate entrances so they had time to get away if the police went to the front door first. When one of them heard the police was coming, they quickly sent word to their friends and comrades, who moved on to the next hiding place.

It wasn't just boys on the hit list; there were girls too. And they had their own tricks and techniques for evading the police. Many of them looked older than they were, and they used that to their advantage by disguising themselves as older family members, wearing head scarves and aprons to complete the effect.

But there were only so many places to hide in the squatter camps. When the children had exhausted their options, they took to sleeping outside instead. There they spent their nights in the bushes, doing what boys and girls do when they're alone in the dark, away from adult eyes.

While it wasn't Owéna's place to get involved in the political side of the conflict, dealing with the sudden increase in teenage pregnancies was very much within her remit as a social worker.

With no medical facilities in the squatter camps except for an occasional mobile clinic, Owéna's main concern was making sure the girls got proper care. She took them to the Knysna hospital, where she left them in the nurses' hands.

In that same hospital, Owéna had given birth to all three of her own children. But she'd done so in the wing for white people; the black girls had to go in through the back entrance to the hospital, to the more crowded wing for non-whites.

One day when Owéna dropped off a pregnant girl for her check-up, she noticed a group of black boys in the emergency room who she recognised from the squatter camps. Some of them had swollen faces, others had blood on their shirts and trousers.

Owéna didn't approve of the violence. For years, she had been trying to show the black people of Knysna that the real way to make change happen was to talk, not fight.

And it worked. The Thembalethu and Vulindlela committees had managed to make a real difference in the past four years, with many of the new water tanks and taps in the squatter camps a direct result of their talks with the mayor.

So it was with real excitement that Owéna took a call

from Mayor Stan Thesen, asking her to help him put together a new official liaison committee.

Inspired by the Thembalethu and Vulindlela committees and their willingness to talk, the mayor wanted the new committee to meet regularly with him and his council to discuss the needs of the black community, and the ways in which the municipality could help.

Owéna gave him the names of people she knew and respected, and who she knew would welcome the opportunity to improve the lives of their people.

While the adults were willing to talk, Owéna could understand why the black children were resorting to violence instead. She'd seen how hard it was for them to get to school, how hard it was for their parents to keep them in school, how frustrating it was when they finally got through school and realised their qualification would never get them the same opportunities as their white countrymen.

They deserved to be angry, Owéna thought. And when you don't have a voice, how else do you express your anger?

Chapter 42

1986

Owéna was livid when she heard the news.

Overnight, several people in the squatter camps had been arrested. She knew most of them; they were prominent people in the black community, shop owners and businessmen. Good, innocent people. Some of them were even members of the mayor's new liaison committee.

Owéna had heard about it from one of their wives, who'd come down to Child Welfare in tears that morning. The woman said the police had hammered on their door at midnight. They had guns, which they pointed in her and her husband's faces, demanding to see receipts for their television and their hi-fi. When her husband failed to produce the receipts, the police accused him of stealing the goods. He was arrested and taken away. The woman was pregnant and had no income of her own.

Her husband wasn't the only one. Over seventy people had been arrested, leaving behind families who had no idea when they'd see their husbands and fathers again.

And it wasn't only men, either. In some homes, husbands

and wives were arrested together, so that their children had to be taken in by neighbours.

For how long, they didn't know.

Owéna stormed in to the Knysna police station and past the officer on reception. She knew exactly where she was going.

She found the lieutenant in his office, behind his desk.

Owéna was shaking, she was so angry.

She demanded the people be released, but the lieutenant was unrepentant.

Those people were troublemakers, he said. Leaders who instigated the unrest and the violence. If the police found some stolen goods in the process of arresting them, that was a bonus. They were always going to be arrested. Their names were on the list. There was a national state of emergency, he said. Didn't Owéna know?

Of course Owéna knew. The national state of emergency had been announced just twenty-four hours before.

There had already been a regional state of emergency in the Western Cape, and for even longer in the Eastern Cape. But with the news that it was going national came new emergency regulations that gave police sweeping powers to control people's movement.

Overnight, it became illegal for black people to congregate in one place, possess any 'threatening documents', tell anyone to go on strike or oppose the government, or boycott shops. Police could restrict township funerals to weekdays, impose curfews, and stop schoolchildren from being outside their classrooms during school hours.

Owéna could see how some of those restrictions were necessary to stop the violence. But as far as she knew, it was only the young people who were getting out of hand. None of the older people she'd spoken to wanted the violence. They just wanted to be heard.

The lieutenant refused to listen. The arrests were entirely lawful under the new emergency regulations, he said. Any suspected instigators could be arrested and detained without trial.

Owéna knew it was true, and left the police station feeling frustrated and helpless. Back at the office, she started making up food parcels for the families who'd been left behind.

The next time Theron went to fetch Johnny and Queenie for work, there were police roadblocks where the road from Dam-se-Bos met the N2. Johnny said they'd been there all night, and the day before that. The people were saying it was to catch anyone on the list who might be trying to get away. But Theron knew it was also to stop any trouble from getting to town.

The police had recently been to Knysna High, where they'd asked for volunteers to guard the school over the weekend. Although the defence force had sent reinforcements from Oudtshoorn, they couldn't be everywhere at once. And the school was an obvious target, as it was the first major public building on the route from Witlokasie to town.

Theron put his name down as a volunteer.

That weekend, Theron joined a group of male teachers who took it in turns to take four-hour shifts to guard the school. But the streets around Knysna High were almost eerily quiet, as was the rest of town, where businesspeople and church-goers were also keeping watch.

The teachers rather enjoyed their civic duty and, while one of Theron's more right-wing colleagues turned up to the school with a shotgun and a revolver, the rest of them turned up with a bottle of wine and a few lamb chops for the *braai*. By the Saturday night they were joined by their female colleagues, who came along for the party.

For most white people in Knysna, life went back to normal soon after the initial excitement of the state of emergency, and news that the town's Oyster Festival would be going ahead was happily received.

But at Child Welfare, Owéna was still dealing with the aftermath of the arrests, helping those families who'd been left without breadwinners in the only way she could.

Owéna and her colleagues drove bakkie-loads of food parcels and clothes up to the squatter camps, always making sure the limited supplies were going to the people in most need. Despite teaming up with World Vision and receiving many donations from Knysna's white and coloured communities, there was only so much to go around. And no one knew when the detainees would be released.

One day, on her way up to the squatter camps to deliver another load of food, Owéna noticed the streets were littered with pamphlets. She stopped to pick one up, feeling the blood rise in her face as she read the message. It was from the security forces, written in Xhosa, English and Afrikaans:

ATTENTION ALL RESIDENTS
WITHOUT WORK YOU CANNOT EAT.

YOUR WORK IS YOUR FUTURE.

WILL THE COMRADES PAY YOU?

CAN THE COMRADES SUPPORT YOUR FAMILY?

DO NOT BE AFRAID OF THE COMRADES.

1986

THE SECURITY FORCES ARE IN COMMAND.
THE SECURITY FORCES WILL PROTECT ANYONE WHO IS
WILLING TO WORK.

She crumpled up the pamphlet and threw it on the floor of the Child Welfare bakkie.

While Owéna did what she could to help the wives of the men who'd been arrested, the wives did what they could to help their husbands.

Seventy-five people in total had been arrested and most of them taken to George, where they were kept in prison. Their wives were allowed to visit them, but with sixty kilometres between them, they knew they needed to find money if they were going to make the journey often.

The community pulled together, putting on concerts and morning markets where they sold old clothes and bottles of homemade ginger beer. From the proceeds, they hired minibuses to take them to George with tubs of soup to keep the detainees nourished, and news from home to keep their spirits up.

As July became August and August became September, the detainees in George started being released: four today, five tomorrow, a few days later another five or so. There was no warning or notice; in one instance, a man's wife had just been to visit him from Knysna when he was told he was free to go. He got home before his wife did.

But when the men came home, many of them found they no longer had jobs. They had been away too long and had come back labelled as troublemakers.

Owéna thought it was disgraceful and went to the mayor, who agreed. Through his liaison committee, Stan Thesen had come to know several of the men as good, upstanding members of the community. He wrote to Knysna's businesses urging them to re-employ the released detainees and stressing that the detentions did not imply that the people were guilty of an offence, or even that a charge would be made against them. The letter went out to supermarkets and sawmills, factories and farms.

Some people got their jobs back, but not all.

Owéna followed up the mayor's letter with phone calls to the employers, pleading with them to take back the workers whose honesty and decency she couldn't emphasise enough. Spurred on by every man and woman she managed to convince, Owéna made more calls, often from home at night when she knew the employers would be with their own families, and so hopefully in a more compassionate frame of mind.

One night, when she dialled the first number, she heard a sound on the line that she could've sworn hadn't been there before.

'Click.'

Chapter 43

Tapped

I can't remember when my parents first told me about our phone being tapped, but it was many years after the fact. Later, it became a quirky story to tell friends and boyfriends when they came over to our house for a *braai*. While waiting for the wood to turn to coals, my father entertained us with stories of phones clicking and mysterious cars following him and my mother to town.

But it looks like it's going to be impossible to prove it. There's nothing about any surveillance in the municipality records, which isn't all that surprising as it probably isn't the kind of thing the town council would've discussed in their meetings. Chances are, they wouldn't have known about it at all.

Even the police had their phones tapped by the security police, according to Lawrence Oliver. He told me the security police came from Mossel Bay to Knysna, where they would disappear into a little room behind the police station that only they had the keys for.

When I ask my parents for more details about the story,

they know as little now as they did then. If there's one thing my mother is sure about, it's that it all started after she confronted the police lieutenant about the arrests and detentions. My father says he wanted to go and punch him, 'that little man with a big rank', for putting my mother on the blacklist.

That same lieutenant was in charge when the Casspirs went into the squatter camps, my father says. He saw the lieutenant go up there with them, the day he first spotted the Casspirs on his way to school.

My mother remembers something else: that she didn't go to the police lieutenant by herself that day. She says her colleague Tia Wessels went with her.

But when I track down Tia, she says she couldn't have gone with my mother, as she'd left Knysna by then. She doesn't doubt that my mother's phone was tapped, though. She says hers was too.

In Tia's case, she says it was her objection to Bongani that got her on the blacklist. After the article in the *Herald* exposed the poor quality of the houses in the temporary township, she took it a step further and threatened to go to the Sunday papers if the authorities didn't do something about it. It wasn't long afterwards that she started hearing the click on her phone. But she was also told about it, she says. By a policeman who said to be careful what she talked about, because her name was on that list.

I'm still hoping to find more concrete proof of the phone-tapping and my father suggests I speak to a relative who used to work for the Bureau of State Security, or BOSS. He might be able to point me in the right direction.

If the security police was South Africa's equivalent of MI5 in the UK or the FBI in the US, BOSS was the equivalent of MI6 or the CIA. I imagine spies and secret missions, but my relative quickly sets me straight. His was an overt rather than a covert role, he says. He was a desk researcher whose job it was to read through overseas newspapers, looking in particular for any news of sporting boycotts and anti-apartheid protests by English students.

He remembers my father mentioning something about our phones being tapped at the time, but more than that he doesn't know. He says the security police were 'cowboys' who did things very differently from BOSS. If they were tapping our phones, the records and transcripts of those conversations should in theory be available, he says. But many of those records got destroyed, 'especially if they were nonsense'. And even if they hadn't been, he has no idea where I might be able to find them. He says the police won't be able to help me either.

With the security police now dissolved and no leads to go on, I have to accept that I might never find the truth.

Chapter 44

1986

When they first became aware of the clicking sound on the phone, Owéna had to stop Theron going straight to the police station and giving the lieutenant a piece of his mind.

She'd heard of some kind of list being compiled by the security police, a list of names of white people they were keeping an eye on. *Kafferboeties* they called them: kaffir brothers. White people who sided, or even just sympathised, with the blacks.

Rumour had it the head of the Black Sash in Knysna was on the list, which didn't surprise Owéna. The Black Sash were very publically taking sides with the black community, informing them of their rights in their arrests and detentions and supporting them in their protests and marches.

As for her own name being on the list, Owéna wasn't fazed. If anything, she was amused at how the security police were wasting their time. She didn't know what they were expecting to hear, but most of the calls she made were to her mother, her sister and her mother-in-law in Cape Town to share the usual news about the kids and their cousins.

After a while Theron stopped taking it seriously too. Every time he phoned someone, he made a point of saying '*Hallo, julle donners van die sekuriteitspolisie*' – Hello, you swine from the security police – before he started his conversation.

And when he and Owéna started noticing two men occasionally following them in their car, they just smiled and waved at the men in the rear-view mirror as they went on their way.

Owéna did wonder why the phone was still clicking even after the detainees had all been released and the unrest in Knysna seemed, for the most part, to be over. Perhaps the security police just hadn't got round to removing the tap from the phone.

If anything, the situation in the squatter camps was more positive than ever. With the detainees released, the mayor's liaison committee was back to meeting every month. As well as the black representatives that Owéna had put forward, the youth were represented too. A couple of Tembelitsha schoolchildren sat on the committee alongside town council members and delegates from the Rotary Club.

Owéna went along to the meetings and left each one feeling confident that things were finally going to get done. There were plans for a new cemetery in Bongani, communal taps in Dam-se-Bos and Witlokasie, and water tanks in Oupad and Jood-se-Kamp. The children's needs were especially high on the agenda, with the town council looking into buying a second-hand bus to transport the children to school, and agreeing to finally install electricity in Tembelitsha's classrooms.

In keeping with Owéna's principle of helping the people to help themselves, the committee made sure they involved the community in making the plans happen. To cover the cost of running the new school bus, the children would have to pay a fare. And the municipality would pay the Tembelitsha schoolchildren to work with its electrical engineer to dig trenches for the power lines at the school.

When good things happened, Owéna made sure the white as well as the black communities knew about it.

So when Thesen's, a local timber factory, donated its old gatehouse as an additional classroom for Mam Tau's school, Owéna organised plenty of fanfare around the event.

Crowds of onlookers, white, black and brown, watched as the gatehouse was lifted, intact, onto a flatbed truck and driven through Knysna and up to Dam-se-Bos where Owéna and Mam Tau were waiting at the school.

But for every success story, there was a setback.

Heavy rains stalled the installation of the taps at Dam-se-Bos. The plans for the new school bus had to be scrapped after parents said they couldn't afford the fares, no matter how heavily subsidised. And the trenches at Tembelitsha were put on hold while the young would-be labourers wrote their exams.

The community got impatient, accusing the liaison committee of making promises it couldn't keep.

The biggest sticking point of all was the new township.

In the thirty years that Knysna's black community had been promised an official township, there was one thing they had always been clear about: they did not want wooden houses.

Most of their shacks were already made from wood and, with so many of those shacks having burned to the ground, they had no desire to move to another wooden house – especially not one they'd have to pay for.

So when an ad appeared in a national newspaper inviting tenders for wooden houses in the 'Umsobomvu' township, the people were furious.

They'd already voiced their concern about the infrastructure. The tar roads that had started to appear on the scraped land were too narrow, they said. Cars would barely be able to pass each other, and almost certainly not buses.

And where had the name 'Umsobomvu' come from? It meant 'rising dawn', but in Nguni – a language not even represented among Knysna's black population, who were predominantly Xhosa.

The people brought these objections to the liaison committee, but there was nothing they could do about the situation. The township fell under the jurisdiction of the provincial administration, not the Knysna Municipality.

The people, not understanding the bureaucracy involved, began to question the liaison committee's credibility. And Owéna noticed, with growing unease, that the people were getting restless once again.

Chapter 45

Elizabeth Koti

I've been watching the news with my parents every night and there's been a recurring theme for the last few days. The service delivery protests are breaking out all over South Africa, like some kind of mass action. News reports from across the country show similar scenes to the ones I saw at the Knysna Municipality, right down to the messages on the placards: 'We vote for 15 years.' 'Enough is enough.' 'We want houses.' 'We want electricity.'

In the *Herald* there's a report about a public meeting in Dam-se-Bos. Elizabeth Koti is pictured looking amazingly defiant for someone who has been receiving threats from the community.

According to the article, it was the second such meeting in the last few weeks after the first 'ended in chaos' following 'noisy protest action', with councillors having to be escorted from the hall by the police.

It looks like the protest action worked. The municipality reportedly went away and reallocated their resources, 'having understood the strong message the people had sent them'.

As a result, Dam-se-Bos will start getting services in about eight weeks, and houses will follow in the next eleven months.

I'm hoping this means the community will be placated now, at least for the time being.

In light of the news, I finally give Elizabeth Koti a call. She sounds in good spirits and remembers me from my previous visit. Yes, she's happy to speak to me again, she says. But not at her office in Dam-se-Bos, not with what's been going on. Maybe we can meet in town; I should give her a call next week.

Despite the newspaper article promising progress, I'm relieved we're not meeting in Dam-se-Bos. The burning road signs are still fresh in my mind.

When I finally get to see Elizabeth Koti, it's at her house in Dam-se-Bos after all. We've had to rearrange our meeting twice, and each time she's changed the venue, from 'somewhere in town' to her office, to, finally, her house.

I hope that means it's safe now.

It's not Elizabeth who opens the door, but a girl of about five or six who runs off to call her. On a sofa, a young black man and woman are watching TV and I join them. I have no idea who they are.

On the screen, a bride's white dress contrasts dramatically with her black skin, her red lips glistening as she steps out the front door of a house and into the sunlight. I recognise that door; it's the same one I've just walked through.

It must be Elizabeth's son's wedding. I know he got married just last weekend; it's why she couldn't see me then. But I never imagined the bride would be getting ready here, in this house with the threat of violence still hanging over it.

When Elizabeth enters the room, the couple turn off the TV and disappear down the hallway without having to be asked.

Elizabeth sinks heavily into an armchair while I fiddle with the cables of the camcorder, anxious not to waste her time. She's an imposing woman and having met her before, I know she doesn't take any nonsense.

I comment on the wedding video, saying it looks like it was an amazing day.

'*Ja*, it was Saturday,' says Elizabeth. 'I'm so tired.'

I'm keen to get straight onto recent events – the toyi-toying and the threats – but I'm also aware that they're not entirely resolved, so I broach the subject hesitantly.

Elizabeth assures me she's fine to talk about it and, with the camcorder set up, she tells me her side of the story.

It's not the first time it's happened, she says. Every time, before the local government elections you see this sort of action in the communities. She's talking about the marches and the threats.

It's political, she says. The people instigating the riots and the violence are those who want to become leaders themselves. They want her position. And with most of her ward still consisting of squatters, she's an easy target.

'The houses are being built,' she says. 'The development is there. But the development didn't start immediately. So those people who want to be in power started spreading rumours.'

According to one of those rumours, Elizabeth used the money earmarked for local development to buy cars, for herself and for her son. Another claimed she'd built her house with the municipality's money.

I ask her about a story I heard recently, that her son's car tyres were slashed.

'Oh, did you hear that?' She laughs, but there's no humour in it.

They would have slashed her tyres, she says, but they couldn't get to her car in the garage. So instead they slashed her son's tyres in the yard outside her house. That was when they said they were going to burn the house.

She always talks about 'they'. Not one person with a name and an address where the police can find him. Just 'they', a faceless crowd of interchangeable people, one as angry as the other.

I ask her whether they actually said that to her, that they were going to burn down her house.

'No, we've got informers,' she says, using a word I've only ever heard associated with the apartheid years in this country. As if she's reading my mind, Elizabeth adds, 'It happened in the past when we were fighting the apartheid government and it's still happening now. It leaks. And when it leaks, it comes to my ears. For my security.'

She got word of the plans in time to involve the police, who came in three vans and stayed outside her house all night.

'They' stayed away.

She's talking about the night before the morning I came up here with my father, and I remember the marks from the burning tyres not far from here. They might have stayed away from her house, but they made a considerable mess all around it.

I ask her how it made her feel, being threatened like that.

'I am traumatised, obviously,' she says. 'They are trauma-tising me.'

She doesn't sound upset. She sounds bitter.

Her tone doesn't surprise me, not when I hear when the

trouble first started. It was barely a week after her husband had died when the first mob tried to toyi-toyi their way to her house.

'I was still sitting in the room, on the mattress,' she says. 'You know in our tradition, you sit there for two weeks until the funeral.'

I do know, but only because my mother told me what Elizabeth would have had to go through after her husband died. In Xhosa culture, in the mourning period immediately after a man's death, his widow must sleep on a mattress on the bedroom floor. She's allowed to leave the bedroom while no one's around, but if any visitors come to pay their respects, she must return to the bedroom and be seated on the mattress before she can see them.

Elizabeth tells me she was still in that period of mourning when she got a text message from an informer. She didn't know who it was; there was no name, just a number.

The message said there had just been a meeting and the people were coming the following morning at eight o'clock to march on her house.

Elizabeth forwarded the message to the police, who were waiting for the rioters when they turned up the following day.

'It was in the middle of the festival,' she says. 'And the festival people were cycling.'

She's referring to Knysna's annual cycle race, the second-biggest draw of the Oyster Festival, after the marathon. Thousands of cyclists from all over the country take part in the race, which passes the townships on the N2, not far from Elizabeth's house.

The police stayed at the N2 junction until the race was finished, so the mob couldn't come over to carry out their threat.

I wonder whether the cyclists noticed the extra police presence, whether any of them caught a glimpse of the rioters. I'm reminded of Lawrence Oliver's tales of girls in shorts and bikini tops walking around town, unaware of the black crowd being held back by police just at the top of the hill.

But that was 1986. The cycle race was two months ago.

I ask Elizabeth if she's scared. Not *was* she scared, *is* she scared. Now. Here.

'No,' she says firmly, then adds: not for herself. But she is worried about her family.

'When they come to throw the petrol bomb into my house, they target me,' she says. 'But I am not going to be the one who's going to burn to death. I've got a mother-in-law here who's seventy-nine years old, and two grandchildren who are staying here. I am younger than my mother-in-law, I know my house. Even if it's dark, I know where the door is and I can be outside. But I wouldn't be able to go and fetch somebody else. So my concern is that those people are going to die because of me.'

Has she considered going to stay somewhere else?

'No', she says, as firmly as before. 'I want to stay here. I am bold enough to stay here. I'm not going to move. I will show them, I'm not going to move. I'm fed up of them.'

She's quiet for a moment, then says it again.

'I'm fed up of them.'

I sense that 'them' no longer refers to the faceless crowds but to the individuals who are inciting them; resentful people with chips on their shoulders and political grudges to bear, who spread rumours and vitriol among the people. Her next words confirm this.

'The leaders of this group are not stupid,' she says. 'But

they mislead the people who don't read and write and don't understand things.'

Despite her determination to stay in her house, Elizabeth has no desire to stay in her job. This is it, she says. At the end of her current term she won't run for councillor again.

But she's worried about what will happen when she stands down.

'They can't all be councillors,' she says. 'In my place is going to be one councillor. And when I monitor them from a distance, I see four of them who want to be in the race. And only one of them can win. It will split them and that is going to cause a problem for them.'

We move on to the struggle years, revisiting some of the topics we touched on the last time I was here. I'm also keen to ask her about David Ngxale.

But first I remind her of Goodman Xokiso. The last time I was here, I didn't know who she was talking about when she mentioned the 'Tatas' child who'd been shot. Now I can tell her about the Truth and Reconciliation reports and the conversations I've had and the conflicting stories I've been told. Stories like the one about the community accusing Esther of selling the child's body to the police.

'I am one of the community who said that,' says Elizabeth, her expression serious.

Her version of the story matches the one I've pieced together myself. The community wanted a comrade's funeral for the boy, but his mother wanted a private burial. So when Esther gave the boy's body to the police and let them bury him in private, the community said she'd sold the body.

'It was the language we took and said, "She sold the body",' says Elizabeth.

Finally, I understand. And with the understanding comes

a pang of pity for Esther Xokiso, the resentful woman who spat so angrily on the floor at the mere mention of the community's accusation, not realising it had been a figure of speech.

We start talking about how the community used to raise money for the struggle, and the black children's involvement in the fundraising efforts. I use the mention of the children as a segue to ask about David Ngxale.

Elizabeth doesn't remember much about him, just that he was involved with a so-called Civic Organisation on the youth side. She says she thinks he was in jail in 1986, during the state of emergency. 'Because the police feel he is the troublemaker, he must be kept there. And his friend ran away, Winile Joyi. Did you meet him?'

It's a name that's come up in a few other interviews. I was briefly introduced to Winile at the municipality when I was going through the archives. He seemed eager to talk, almost pushy. He gave me his business card but I haven't been in touch.

I want to keep talking about David and steer the conversation back to him: does she know him?

Yes, she knows him, Elizabeth says, although she didn't work with him closely back then.

'They were leaders of the community,' she says, 'and we were below. He was working at a higher level.'

She reckons it could be true that David was targeted by the police. There was an *impimpi*, a police informer, who lived near him in Jood-se-Kamp.

'The police believed if they could get David and Winile, the whole group would be quiet,' she says. 'And that was not true.' There's a new zeal in her voice as she carries on.

'Even if they did take David and lock him up for two years, that was not going to stop us operating the way we wanted to operate until the government released us from the oppression. That was not going to stop us. Because somebody must feel the pain.'

I imagine what she must have been like then, this head-strong woman fighting against the oppression.

When Elizabeth walks me to my car, I'm relieved to see the tyres are fine.

I ask her if she's going to be OK.

Yes, she assures me.

'They can't get to me. They can try, but I'm not going anywhere.'

Chapter 46

1987

The Tembelitsha schoolchildren had learned a new word: 'demands'. And they were putting together a whole list of them to take to the mayor's liaison committee. Owéna tried to teach them a different word: 'grievances', which was what she put at the top of the list when she typed it up.

It was Owéna's idea to do the list. Having realised that the schoolchildren were getting angry again, she'd sat down with a group of them to get their frustrations down on paper. There were many.

Conditions at Tembelitsha had gone from bad, to briefly better, to worse. The 'briefly better' period had been when the principal built on some extra classrooms two years before. But by 1987, Tembelitsha was full to bursting, with almost nine hundred students in the small Witlokasie school and its satellite schools in Bongani and Dam-se-Bos. And there were only twenty teachers to teach them all.

The house that Theron, Doug and Johnny had built for the teachers four years before, the one that was only ever meant to last three years, was still standing and fully occupied.

And with the new black township still under construction, there was once again nowhere for new teachers to live. As a result, the school was in chaos. The children summed it up in their list of grievances. There was no headmaster. There were no textbooks. Teachers were drunk at school. Windows were getting smashed. Chairs were being stolen.

Owéna took the list to the mayor's liaison committee. But without funding from the government, there was little the local authorities could do. The municipality had been doing everything within its power to supply water and sanitation in the squatter camps, scraping together funds from other budgets. But the school needed a considerably bigger investment, and the government was refusing to put money into it when there were plans to build a school in the new, official township.

Owéna could understand the town council's dilemma, but she wasn't going to accept it. If it was money from the government they needed, she was going to help them get it.

Owéna wrote to the African Scholars' Fund.

Set up to give financial assistance to specific children, selected on a case-by-case basis, the fund wasn't likely to give money towards an entire school like Tembelitsha. And Owéna wasn't expecting it to. What she was hoping, however, was that the fund could help to create awareness of Tembelitsha's plight.

It worked.

Not long after she wrote to the fund, two of its trustees, including founder Dr Margaret Elmsworth, came to Knysna to inspect the black school.

After two days of touring Tembelitsha and its satellite schools, Dr Elmsworth outlined her findings in a report to the mayor and the town clerk.

286

In our sixteen years of working in black education, Mrs Livingstone and I consider that the Knysna schools are among the worst, if not the worst, in the Cape Province. It is inconceivable that 180 children can be taught by two teachers in tiny makeshift wooden shacks, or that standard four [grade six] children can read their books in the dank, dark church hall at Tembelitsha.

The only good thing about the school, she wrote, was the view.

Dr Elmsworth ended her report with a remark aimed directly at the local authorities, saying that 'the contrast of luxury boating and tourism with the squalor of the black schools is a serious indictment of the management of the area.'

The mayor and the town clerk didn't take the criticism personally. They took it to the government as evidence that the black schools needed more funding.

Four months later, the Ministry of Education and Development Aid agreed to supply two prefabricated class-rooms and extra bucket toilets for Tembelitsha. And the Bongani school was upgraded to standard four, so that fewer children had to walk all the way to Witlokasie.

Encouraged by the result, Owéna decided to take other matters in her own hands too.

While at a welfare congress in Johannesburg, she'd heard that a national Afrikaans newspaper, *Rapport*, was donating minibuses to charities, provided they made a convincing enough case.

Owéna got writing. And when she didn't hear back immediately, she got calling. After months of badgering the paper, she convinced them to donate a minibus to Child Welfare to ferry the Tembelitsha children to and from school.

But Child Welfare couldn't afford the cost of running the bus. And Owéna knew from the town council's aborted effort to supply a bus service that the black parents couldn't afford to pay a fare, either.

Owéna went to the town council. She'd got a bus, she said. A brand-new one. But it was useless if all it did was sit at the Child Welfare offices. Was there any way they could help with funds for petrol? The town council went one better, supplying not just the funds but a driver too.

Owéna wasn't alone in wanting to help Tembelitsha. With small victories like the *Rapport* minibus making the local paper, the rest of Knysna was becoming more aware of the black school and the difficulties it faced. And soon Knysna's charities, clubs and businesses were stepping in.

The Round Table chased the government for funding to pay for the electricity at Tembelitsha. A local company donated a film projector for fundraising film nights. And the Black Sash, along with a group called the Concerned Women of Knysna, arranged for textbooks to be collected in the Eastern Cape.

One by one, the grievances on the schoolchildren's list were being ticked off.

But the community's biggest grievance remained unanswered.

What was happening with the new township?

Chapter 47

1987–8

Work on Knysna's first official black township had come to a virtual standstill. At least it now had a name that met the black community's approval: *Khayalethu*. It was the one concession the government's provincial administration had been willing to make in the whole controversial project: to let the people choose the name for the township after they rejected *Umsobomvu*.

Owéna liked the new name and its meaning: 'our home'. Indeed, if the people's reaction to the new name were anything to go by, it would seem as if they were warming to the idea of the new township.

But, in truth, most of them were in no hurry to move there. After their arguments against wooden houses had fallen on deaf ears, the people found out that the only school in the new township would be yet another primary school, when they'd been crying out for a high school all those years. Once again, they felt their needs had been ignored.

Even those people who did want to move to Khayalethu, those who longed for flushing toilets and lights in their homes, wouldn't be going anywhere for a while. All seven hundred and eighty plots of land, complete with access to water, sewage facilities and electricity, had been standing empty for two years.

With not a house in sight, rumours spread among the black community that the land wasn't even going to be used for a township anymore.

Owéna knew the truth from the liaison committee meetings, but it wasn't her place to communicate it to the people.

Not that she wanted to, either. It wasn't good news.

After years of analysing the proposed township area, the provincial administration had found that the soil quality was so poor and the slopes so steep that not all of the plots could be developed. And where it was possible to build, it would be so expensive to make the houses safe that they'd be unaffordable for the black people unless they were heavily subsidised. It looked like wooden houses on stilts were the only option, but when exactly they'd be finished, or even started, no one knew.

When the provincial administration did eventually communicate the news at a public meeting in Witlokasie, Owéna went along to listen.

Theron wasn't in Knysna at the time. He was in Cape Town marking matric exam papers during the school holidays, a task he'd signed up for to bring in some extra money. The two youngest children had gone with him for a holiday at their grandparents', while the oldest, who had just turned sixteen, spent the long break from school at a friend's beach house.

In Cape Town, Theron watched the news with his parents while the children played snooker upstairs. There had been explosions in Boksburg and Brakpan near Johannesburg. There had also been a bomb in Paarl, just forty-five kilometres from where his parents lived in the Strand.

Throughout 1988 the violence had been getting worse. And it was no longer the sticks and stones violence of the '86 unrest, when it was black against police. Now it was car bombs and limpet mines and grenades in bars and clubs and restaurants and train stations.

Now it was terrorism.

The whole country was on high alert, and Knysna was no different. Worried about bombs, the Knysna Municipality had removed all flower boxes from the main street, and there were no longer any rubbish bins outside the post office.

Back at Knysna High, Theron had been having to interrupt his lessons for regular bomb drills. But the one or two times the evacuations were in response to 'actual' tip-offs, it was almost certainly a schoolchild trying to get out of a maths or economics test.

Compared with the rest of the country, Knysna still felt a relatively safe place to be white.

But for how long? thought Theron as he watched the bloodied faces of survivors on the news.

Owéna didn't know much about the political goings-on behind the scenes in Knysna's squatter camps. All she knew was that the black community was becoming more politically aware. And that a kind of in-fighting had started among them. The black members of the mayor's liaison committee had started to resign, giving in to pressure from their community, who criticised them for being all talk and no action.

Meanwhile, the government's provincial administration had started its own *skakelkomitee*, the Afrikaans name for 'liaison committee' by which it was known. It recruited some black people to sit on the committee, and they were soon accused by the rest of the community of being pawns in the apartheid government's plans to herd people into townships.

All the politics and squabbling made Owéna uncomfortable, and she distanced herself from the various rallies, marches and talks that were happening more frequently.

But when she heard of the public meeting in Witlokasie where the new township would be discussed and the people informed of their options, Owéna's curiosity got the better of her.

With no Theron around to stop her, she took the Child Welfare bakkie and headed up to Witlokasie.

The Tembelitsha classroom was packed. Owéna was pleased to see so many people taking an interest in the plans for the township, even if they didn't necessarily agree with it. At least they were having a say in their future. But as soon as the provincial administration started talking, the disruption started.

At the back of the room, a group of men Owéna didn't recognise shouted objections and abuse. There was anger in their eyes. But there was something else, too. Fire.

The representatives from the administration were visibly unnerved. But they pressed on, explaining the people's options for housing in the new township.

There were three ways of getting a house in Khayalethu, they said. People could buy a fully serviced plot and apply for a loan to build their own home. If they couldn't afford that, they could apply for a special plot with more rudimentary services. That would be free for the first year, then there'd be a basic rent and service charges to pay. And if that was still outside their reach, they could put their name on the list to buy one of the subsidised houses that would be built for them.

Wooden houses, the men called out from the back.

And what if the people can't keep up the payments?

Whatever answers the speakers came up with, the men had a counter-argument. And their voices were getting louder.

Owéna noticed that some of the black people in the room looked as uncomfortable as she felt. She recognised most of those people, and knew that they'd wanted the new township for a long time, especially the older ones who just wanted a flushing toilet and electricity to make their lives a bit easier.

But other people were nodding in agreement with the dissenters at the back. The men were stirring the crowd, encouraging them to stand up and defy the government. All around Owéna, people were turning around to look at them.

Wooden houses burn, said the men from the back.

Owéna felt a chill. It didn't sound like they were merely stating a truism. It sounded like a threat.

And for the first time, Owéna felt scared.

Chapter 48

Winile Joyi

Winile Joyi is nothing like David Ngxale. Whereas I had a hard time imagining soft-spoken David at the forefront of anything, much less an uprising, Winile is much easier to picture with a loudhailer in his hand. He's all about the politics, peppering his rapid-fire monologue with references to 'comrades' and 'the system' and 'mass democratic action'. He has even invented his own word to describe what he and David were doing back in the apartheid years: 'conscious-tising'.

Where David had sadness in his eyes, Winile has fire.

What soon becomes clear is that, for whatever reason – be it political self-promotion or a genuine desire to record history for posterity – Winile is willing to confess to past acts and actions that others have only implied or skirted around. Acts like the incitement and intimidation of people, including children, who wouldn't join in the marches and rallies of the struggle.

We're in a quiet coffee shop and every so often I glance at a young white woman at a table near us. Winile is speaking very loudly, but the woman seems too engrossed in her book to care.

Winile tells me how he used to coerce people into marching. 'We used to say, "If you're not on this bus, you must be aware of the wheel – when it returns it might hit you on the way." The tactics and the things that we used to say in the loudhailing . . . Some of them might seem intimidating to other people. People wanted to be part of it, but they were afraid.'

And he'd rather the people were afraid of the comrades than of the police.

Winile even admits that the Knysna Civic Organisation, or 'Civics', of which he was chairman and David was secretary, gave the orders to burn down a clinic in Khayalethu because 'it was not the people's clinic'.

It was all part of 'making the country ungovernable', he says, quoting the ANC's objective of the time. 'It was one of the tactics. We wanted to cripple the government in a way to get the attention.'

He says they knew actions spoke louder than words. Especially when the municipality was taking so long to make decisions. That's why he and David formed a Mass Action Committee, organising marches and rallies 'to vent our feelings about the treatment that we have. Because if we were to do that as an individual or write memos to the municipality, there will be just paperwork and correspondence, but not actual action.'

I know that's true at least in part, having seen some of the paperwork and correspondence in the municipality archives. The amount of red tape in apartheid South Africa was quite astonishing.

Winile says one of the Civics' jobs was to distribute

anti-government propaganda from SANCO, their parent organisation. It would have been illegal under state of emergency regulations.

He would have denied it then, but Winile now admits freely that he and David were the organisers and instigators. As a result, they were constantly being chased and harassed, he says. For being 'at the forefront'.

The most contentious issue at the time was Khayalethu, which the Civics were actively trying to stop people moving to.

I ask him outright whether they used scare tactics to put people off moving, like threatening to burn down their houses if they did.

'I have to be honest with you, you know,' he says before answering my question: 'Yes!'

They had to, he says. Because people in Knysna 'were not so much conscioustised politically.'

Chapter 49

1988

When Theron came back from Cape Town, he sat Owéna down. He didn't like her going up there to the black areas any more, not with the things that were going on in the rest of the country. He knew the people cared about her, but there were other people, malicious people, who were coming in to Knysna from other places and causing trouble. He didn't want to raise the children alone.

Owéna didn't argue, having seen and heard some of those people first-hand. But she did think. And she remembered.

She remembered how nervous she'd been about her first day at Child Welfare, and how worried she'd been that she wouldn't be up to the job.

She remembered the moment she realised she and her colleagues couldn't eat in the same restaurant, and the embarrassment that she'd never realised it before.

She remembered the looks on the crèche children's faces when their feet touched the sea for the first time.

She remembered Queenie crying as she watched two men throw her bed on the back of a truck. And the sagging, rotting walls of Queenie's new house in Bongani. And the hillside graveyard where the coffins washed open in the rain.

She remembered the sound of the Vulindlela and Thembalethu committees singing as they danced with their sweaty coins and crumpled banknotes towards the table with the name *Nobantu*.

She remembered the heat of the burning cars around her as she drove into the squatter camps during the riots. The cries of 'Amandla!' The raised fists. The sticks and stones.

She remembered the ink-black eyes of the stranger who asked her why she wasn't scared to be up there among the black people. And the moment at the recent meeting when she realised she was.

But she also remembered realising something else at the meeting.

Listening to the men at the back of the room standing up for their rights, she knew the people had found their voice.

They didn't need her any more.

A job ad in the *Herald* caught Owéna's eye.

SANEL, the South African National Epilepsy League that had a care home in Knysna, needed a full-time social worker.

Owéna knew the social worker who'd been at the home since it had opened three years before. She'd never been up there herself, but it was just a short detour from her usual route to Witlokasie, where she was due to go the following morning anyway.

Theron listened to Owéna as she reasoned with herself, thoughts spilling out in words. Wasn't it a strange coincidence that the job should come up just then, when she was thinking of leaving Child Welfare? What if it was meant to be?

It wouldn't hurt to pop in on her way to Witlokasie the next morning, would it? Just to have a look around?

Theron didn't answer, knowing he didn't need to.

The following morning, Owéna got in the bakkie after a night of little sleep. She had an hour before she had to be in Witlokasie. Plenty of time to stop by SANEL.

But when she turned the key in the ignition, the bakkie's engine gave a lazy, laboured whine before cutting out completely.

She sighed. The bakkie had been acting up all week, refusing to start. She gave up and called Theron to come and help for the fourth morning in a row, knowing from experience that if she were to keep trying, she'd only flood the engine.

After three tries, Theron got the engine running and Owéna was on her way.

It was only a ten-minute drive to SANEL, but Owéna's nerves made it feel much longer. She could hear her heart beating as she buzzed the intercom to be let in through the electric gate.

Anne, Owéna's social worker friend, was happy to see her – even more so when she heard the reason behind Owéna's impromptu visit. She was very sad to leave SANEL, said Anne. But her husband had a new job in the Eastern Cape, and they were moving soon.

Anne showed Owéna around the care home, introducing her to the staff and the residents they looked after. Some of the staff were black or coloured, but all of the residents were white.

In the corridor, a man wearing a thick plastic helmet smiled at them and Owéna noticed he was missing two front teeth. In the sick bay, nurses counted out pills into flip-top organisers labelled 'William', 'Heidi' and 'Howard'. In a large dining room, breakfast dishes were being cleared off tables covered in bright, laminated tablecloths. A silent piano stood in the corner of the room, waiting for the next opportunity to entertain.

A woman with a limp arm shuffled over to tell them her mother was coming the next morning to take her home for Christmas. Just one more sleep to go.

There was a warmth in the place and the people that made Owéna feel at home.

Anne explained that the job was mainly to keep the residents happy and active. She'd been doing that through supervised activities like knitting and rattan weaving, and regular walks and exercises. There was also a fair bit of peace-keeping required, as short tempers and sensitive natures often led to tears and even fisticuffs.

Another part of the job, said Anne, was to keep in touch with the residents' families. But sadly some of them just didn't want to know, seeing the home as a depository for a problem they couldn't face. Christmas was an especially sad time, she said, as there was always a handful of residents with nowhere to go.

Owéna left SANEL feeling moved by the stories she'd heard and the people she'd met. But driving into Witlokasie, she was again reminded of everything she'd be leaving behind.

They'd come so far, she thought. Through the windows at Tembelitsha, she saw the new ceiling lights in classrooms that were once so dark, the children could barely see their own writing. Across the road, a group of preschool children played outside a house where a mother had started her own crèche, one of several trained crèche mamas who were using their initiative to earn an income from their new skills.

At a water tank, a group of women filling up their drums turned to wave at Owéna as she drove past. A child ran after the bakkie, his bare feet white from the dirt road. And all of them called out to her: *Nobantu!*

She was still thinking of that child when she spoke to Theron that night. What should she do? But Theron insisted it had to be her own decision.

The next morning when she got in the bakkie to leave for work, Owéna realised it didn't have to be her choice. If the job at SANEL was fate, she would leave it to fate to make the decision.

She closed her eyes. If she managed to start the bakkie on her first attempt, she would take it as a sign that she was meant to leave Child Welfare.

She put the key in the ignition and held her breath.

Chapter 50

Goodbyes

I'm packing up my last few things when my mother calls from downstairs to say it's time to go. My father is getting anxious; there are lots of roadworks on the way to the airport and he doesn't want me to miss my flight.

I pull the last few photos off the wall in my old bedroom and stuff them in my hand luggage, the crèche children staring at me with their big, milky eyes from the bottom of my wheelie case.

On the way out, my mother hands me a bag of dried mango, *biltong* and *drywors*. I stuff it in my handbag without looking at her, knowing we'll both cry if I do. She locks the kitchen door behind us, and I find myself wondering if she and my father will be safe in this house with its lack of fence or gate or dog, in this country with all the grudges it still bears.

My father is already in the car, the rest of my luggage packed in the boot. He shouldn't be doing any heavy lifting, not since a heart valve replacement a few years ago, but he still insists on packing the car. We don't do it right, he says.

My mother puts a cassette tape in the player with its removable face, and classical music soothes out of the speakers next to me.

As we turn onto the N2, I look back towards Hornlee with its two-storey houses overlooking the Knysna Lagoon – what was once a coloured township, now home to white and black as well as brown.

Heading towards town, we pass the Knysna Provincial Hospital where I was born in the white wing, while Queenie had to give birth in the wing for black people at the back. The whole hospital is now open to all races, but most white people choose to use the newer private hospital nearby.

Across the road is the building where Stepping Stones used to be, where I once made pictures from raw pasta and paint, and where Lesley Satchel taught the crèche mamas to do the same. It's home to a new nursery school now, and I watch a black mother dropping off her daughter, pigtailed and pretty in a blue dress.

The N2 takes us past the Knysna Waterfront with its yachts and its restaurants, where tourists of all colours and various nationalities amble around carrying bags of gifts and mementoes of their trip to 'the heart of the Garden Route'. I realise that, for the first time in many years, I don't feel like one of them.

My mother points out where Jimmy's Killer Prawns used to be, and I let her repeat the story of how it was the vet's surgery years ago, even though I've heard it twice before. I'm looking out the window on the other side, at Salt River, the place that Vivien called home until one day it wasn't any more. Now it's full of guest houses vying for the passing cars' attention with signs displaying their rates.

Over the White Bridge, up the hill, and Knysna disappears from view.

George Airport is tiny and check-in is quick, making the goodbyes both frustratingly and mercifully short. My mother and I cry. My father sniffs and looks away.

Tomorrow they'll just be two voices on the other end of the phone again.

I hug my mother and walk away, turning around just once for one last wave. My mother's nose is red and her eyes wet, her arms hugging her chest, my father's arm around her shoulders. The goodbyes are always hard. I have no idea when I'll be back to visit, just that next time it'll only be for two weeks, maybe three, the hellos and goodbyes far too close together.

I leave South Africa with as many questions as answers, not just about the past, but about the future.

Will our nation ever be colour-blind? Will the violence ever end? I think back to the township houses with their burglar bars and the protests and the burning Tembelitsha sign. The violent break-ins in my parents' neighbourhood. The threats against Elizabeth Koti.

But then I remember the Tembelitsha children singing that hymn with their eyes closed, and the face of the little black boy leading his classmates at the once-white primary school, and the crèche children belting out *Nkosi Sikelel' iAfrika*.

If it's down to them, I think we're going to be OK.

Epilogue

1994

Owéna turned left at Percy Mdala High School, named after the man who once carried black children across a river so they could get to school. Next door stood the Johnson Tatas community hall, named after the boy shot dead by police during the unrest of '86.

It was eight years since Owéna left Child Welfare, but her new job still took her up to the townships sometimes. In her role as social worker at SANEL, she did outreach work in Knysna's black and coloured townships, educating people about epilepsy. In the black communities, especially, there was much superstition around the condition, with rumours abounding that fits were caused by evil spirits.

But Owéna wasn't in Khayalethu for work that day. She was there to see Queenie's new house, just across the road from the Percy Mdala school.

Queenie took the cake from Owéna with a gap-toothed smile, and Owéna felt a twinge of guilt that she hadn't stopped by sooner. It was over a year since Queenie stopped working for her.

Queenie gave Owéna a grand tour. As they went from room to room, Owéna complimented Queenie on her rugs and her cupboards, her bathroom and her beds. When Owéna recognised a table or chair she'd given Queenie years before, she complimented her on how good it looked in its new home.

Owéna looked at her ex-employee and friend, and thought how happy she was for her. Especially as she knew what Queenie, Tiny and the other residents of Khayalethu had been through to get their houses.

The first government-subsidised houses in Khayalethu were finally built in 1990: wooden houses, on stilts. But they were constructed so poorly, there were gaps between the planks where the wind whistled through. On particularly gusty days, the houses swayed on their stilts.

For a while, many of the people who'd put their names down for those houses refused to move. Those who still considered moving were intimidated by the Civics, who threatened to burn down their houses if they did.

Eventually some people did move to Khayalethu, in secret, at night. But many houses stayed empty and were vandalised, their windows smashed and their doors broken off their hinges.

The authorities had no choice but to give the houses away.

Less controversial were the plots of land where people could build their own brick houses. Queenie had had her eye on one of those plots for years. A little house with a view, she told Tiny. That was all she wanted.

For Queenie and Tiny, the pull of Khayalethu became a push when their house in Bongani burned down after a candle fell over.

Owéna remembered the night well. She and Theron had

rushed up there to find Queenie barely able to speak as she watched the charred land where her house had been.

Theron helped Tiny rebuild their house, laying concrete foundations to make it stronger. But Tiny had had enough of Bongani, and started making enquiries about the land in Khayalethu before the roads in the township were even finished.

From his pension and Queenie's wages, Tiny saved twenty rand here, twenty rand there until he could afford the down payment on not just one plot, but two next to each other. Having lived on top of his neighbours for so many years, Tiny wanted to keep them at a friendly distance in the future. He also had a plan for the extra plot: he would build a second house, where their children could live when they were older.

By the time they were laying the foundations, Queenie and Tiny found out they didn't have to pay the money they still owed. People had complained about having to pay for the land when the wooden houses were free. In a final admission of defeat, the provincial government gave the land away for free, too.

Owéna stood in the back yard looking at the view while Queenie fetched them two chairs from the house. It was only a partial view, obscured by another house and some trees, but it was a view nonetheless.

Owéna looked out towards the lagoon that was actually an estuary, and the island where she'd once taken those children who had never seen the sea.

Queenie emerged from the house with a plastic chair in each hand and for a while they sat in silence, admiring the view.

Owéna spoke first, asking Queenie if she voted in the recent election.

Ja, said Queenie. She and Tiny both.

That's good, said Owéna.

She thought of how much things had changed in the time since she'd left Child Welfare. Nelson Mandela was free, the ANC unbanned and the state of emergency lifted. And after the country's first ever democratic election, Mandela was the new president of South Africa.

In Knysna, the municipality had become a model local authority for being one of the first to integrate white, coloured and black.

Owéna was happy for the black people. But, despite all the change and excitement she'd missed out on experiencing first-hand, she had no regrets about leaving Child Welfare when she did.

The people at SANEL needed her in a way that the black people had stopped doing towards the end.

Yes, the issues at the care home sometimes seemed trivial compared to those in the squatter camps. But to the residents, those issues were just as real. They too were ostracised, except it was for their mental disability instead of the colour of their skin. And she cared about them just as much as she'd cared about the black community in her time at Child Welfare.

Like the black people, they even had a name for her.

They didn't call her *Nobantu*.

They called her Mother.

Where are they now?

March 2019

My mother finally retired in 2013, at the age of sixty-eight. She now spends much of her time helping my father with his woodwork, having finally reached his standard of sanding.

Johnny still works for my parents one day a week. He finally got his RDP house in 2017.

Sadly, several of the people I interviewed for this book have since died. Esther Xokiso, David Ngxale, Lois Bubb, Gillian Carter, Amy Matungana, Shepherd Magadla, Zola Plaatjies, Wiekie Smit and Jack Matjolweni. All of them died from natural causes, except for David Ngxale, who was killed in a car accident on the N2 highway.

Acknowledgements

Ever since my mother begrudgingly agreed to be the subject of this book, she and my father have helped and supported me in too many ways to mention here. For your endless love and encouragement, *dankie Ma en Pa*. I'm so proud to be your daughter.

To Alfonso Perez, thank you for stirring the memories and reminding me where I came from. As your land called you back, so did mine.

Thank you also to all the Dark Angels who were there in Aracena when I wrote what is now the prologue to this book. To John, Jamie and Stuart, for helping me find my own voice after so many years of writing in the voices of others. And to the rest of the Angels: had it not been for your reaction to those first 600 words, I might never have written the other 80,000.

A special thank you to three of you in particular: Gordon

Kerr, for the early introductions and advice. Claire Bodanis, for reading – and so vocally loving – the very different first and third drafts. And Martin Lee, for the emotional words in Spain and the practical thoughts in London.

To David Varela, my now ex-husband but no less of a friend: thank you for the space and encouragement to go off to South Africa for three months, the daily phone calls while I was there and the constant support after I got back – the tireless readings and advice, and ultimately the introduction to Carina UK when I'd all but given up.

To Hannah Westland, thank you for helping me push the early drafts. You were right.

To Lucy Gilmour and the team at Carina; Nia Beynon, Darren Shoffren and Belinda Toor at Harper Collins; and Nyiko Mthembi and the team at Jonathan Ball: thank you for believing in my story and setting it free, in more ways than one.

So many people gave me practical help and advice along the way, notably at the Knysna Library, the University of Cape Town Libraries, the Knysna Municipality and the Land Claims Commission. Back in London, thank you to David Bodanis and Kate Rizzo for advising me on the paperwork side of publishing. And in New York, thank you Kathy Robbins for giving your time so generously.

To Joe Hunter, thank you for listening.

To Martin Hennessey, thank you for giving me the coaching and the confidence to get to the heart of people's stories in situations that were often far outside my comfort zone.

Finally, thank you to everyone who shared your memories. You and my parents *are* this book.

Vivien Paremoer, Ronnie Davidson, Bukelwa Mthatshana, Bongi Mkwakwa, Rhoda Hendricks, Elizabeth Koti, Lesley Satchel, Mrs Martin and Mr Guga at Tembelitsha, Rob Stoker at Knysna Primary, Trish Eustice at Knysna High, Victoria Sigcu, Piet van Eeden, Headman Xokiso, Winile Joyi, Lawrence Oliver, Paula Witney, Ben Demengo, Tia Wessels, Johnny Oliphant, and my brothers Francois and Rudolph.

And to those who shared their stories, but didn't live to read this: Shepherd Magadla. David Ngxale. Esther Xokiso. Lois Bubb. Amy Matungana. Zola Plaatjies. Gillian Carter. Wiekie Smit. Jack Matjolweni. And Queenie Mthatshana.

I hope I've done your memory proud.